FIFTEENTH CENTURY ENGLAND

FIFTEENTH CENTURY ENGLAND

PERCIVAL HUNT

UNIVERSITY OF PITTSBURGH PRESS

CONTENTS

FIFTEENTH
CENTURY
ENGLAND

BEGINNING

At the end, as I read over the full manuscript, it seems to me I may have kept saying that the people of the 1400's are very far-away.

I had not aimed at separation. I had in mind the opposite. I wanted to bring close—by facts and discussion—those so faraway from us but through whom we have come to be what we are. We have gone an immeasurable road since 1400. I wanted to show that those alive then were our intimate creators.

Without a sense of the past, living is likely to be what Shakespeare called "traveling abed"—traveling asleep; a going on in time and action without much understanding or pleasure or anxiety; without the gain of seeing the interplay of new and old, of like and unlike, of repetitions and surprise.

"Behold, I shew you a mystery," St. Paul wrote to his friends at Corinth. He showed; but he did not try to explain what was beyond his sight. Surely, there is no greater earthly mystery than a person, or an age in history, and any explanation of them is broken and dimly seen. Yet—I think—it is worth while to write about them, even though, at the end, there still is left a mystery.

1

CHURCH

The Church and the People

Town and country—all the people in them and all matters under the sky, however scattered and unlike—joined within the universality of the Church. It held the one faith. It was the guide into eternity and the way to happiness on earth. Life was to be controlled by it. That was a truth reverently and universally accepted. That much was sure.

To fifteenth-century people a man outside the Church was "desolately alone." This life on earth was brief and unsubstantial—a penance, a shadow, a grain of sand. Yet—with startling contrast—to both Church and people, living did become at times an intense delight, worth emphasis and expression. Churchmen and laity wore at times the rough garments of humility, but the Church did express itself in scarlet and purple, and the King's uncle, Earl Rivers, over his hair-cloth shirt shone with the colors and caprices of the court. A queen rode to her coronation in cloth of silver and wearing a wreath of rubies—"a woman clothed with the sun."

The Church was part of every interest in England—laws, schools, trade, building, travel, the pageants: such pageants as the York cycle which was the business of the whole town, and used five hundred or six hundred townsmen as actors.

Everywhere in the towns the power of the Church was visible. Ecclesiastical buildings impressed themselves upon the street, and set the skyline. Church lands dominated in the country. All day church bells rang. Canonical time—*prime, nones, vespers,* and the rest—named the hours and gave a pattern to the day. Feasts of

3

the Church and Saints' Days put their marks on the year: Easter, Whitsuntide, Lady Day, All Souls' Day, Christmas.

The way men talked—their pronunciation, their words, turns of phrase, rhythms, pauses, and forms of sentence, all the color and tone of usual English speech—echoed the sounds and substance and structures of the Church's language, English and Latin. The prose and poetry of the century (and for that matter of the sixteenth and seventeenth) are proof of the effect. The Church helped bring the astonishing vigor and grace and exactness of expression which was in fifteenth-century talk, sermons, chronicles, letters, books of every sort, and even in wills and public records and laws. Naturally, we know this human reality best from what was best written— *Mallory*, Caxton's books, *Coverdale*, *Erasmus*, and other classic prose; but it is in the Paston letters, which are not literary, and in the writing of men and women half-remembered or quite forgotten—Colet, Archbishop Rotherham of York, Richard Pace, Thomas Betson—and on thousands of faded pages.

Labor unions and businesses—the guilds and City Companies—seen one way are part of the Church. By title a guild was *The Holy Mystery of,* perhaps, *the Blessed Trinity, the Virgin, All Angels.* Guilds gave stained glass to the churches, statues and porches and gates and whole chapels, land (though most often one person gave land), and supported the Church and endowed its hospitals and its schools. All over England in the 1400's, as wealth came from trade or officeholding or inheritance, churches were being built "to the greater glory of God." York finished the splendid and lovely Minster in 1472. At Bristol, in the middle of the century, the miracle of St. Mary Redcliff was being completed by William Canynges, merchant of the town and four times mayor. Norwich, made rich by the wool trade, had thirty-eight churches, more than any other town but London, and by proportion of numbers more than London. York—thirteen thousand people or so—had fifty churches inside its white stone walls and nine outside. Stratford, by 1460, completed the church of the Holy Trinity on the bank of the Avon. In town and country, from the Scottish border to the Channel, and east and west, everywhere, churches were built.

To build a bridge or a road might be counted an act of piety. It was, truly, service to God and men—and to the Church. Such building is classed as good works along with the much-approved giving to the sick, to prisoners and the very poor, and to penny-less students. For the last moments of the man who had done such

4

charity God would send St. Michael Archangel, his very self, to deliver that man from torments of the eager fiends. *Piers Plowman* tells as God's promise:

> . . .ich shall send yow, my-selue, seynt Michel myn Angel
> That no deuel shal yow dere [torment]. . .in youre deyinge
> And sende youre soules ther ich my-selfe dwelle.

Chapels were part of some bridges. London Bridge had one on it, a two-story chapel. Over the Ouse River at York was a chapel and a council hall; and at Rotherham, forty miles south of York, there was a chantry-chapel of "stone well wrought." At Bedford, the bridge, removed in 1765, had the town jail on it (where Bunyan wrote *Pilgrim's Progress*) and a chapel. At St. Ives, fifteen miles from Cambridge, the "fine, old bridge" still has a tall "chantry-chapel (now a dwelling) on the central pier." At Wakefield in the north was, Leyland wrote in 1533, a "fair bridge of stone of nine arches, under which runneth the river of Calder, and on the east side of this bridge is a right goodly chapel of our Lady." By a charter of Edward III (1358) two priests were "for ever to perform Divine service in [the] Chapel of St. Mary newly built on the bridge at Wakefield." The King endowed the chantry—today, still a beautiful building—with ten pounds a year, a generous provision, three times that of most such gifts. In France there was, among many, the chapel on the *pons d' Avignon* of the nursery song. Bridges were, at times, consecrated to a saint—London Bridge was, to St. Thomas; and the bridge at Stratford-la-Bow, to St. Catherine. A holy hermit might live beside a bridge approach, or in a corner of its gates or towers.

The date of a document or a letter often was told by naming the Saint's Day or the Church Feast on which it was written. A contract was drawn in 1422 for a "bridge of stone over the waters of Swale at Catterwick . . . of two piers, two land abutments, and three arches." It is required that the work shall "be fully performed in all parts and wholly ended [holy endyed] by the Fest of Seint Michille ye Arcangelle quik [when] yt shalle fall in ye yere of Our Lorde Gode M¹ᵉccccxxv." The Pastons were fifteenth-century Norfolk gentry, men and women who were landowners, lawyers, businessmen, students at college, minor officials at court, and the wives and mothers and sisters of these, and the servants of them all. They wrote many letters in the last two-thirds of the 1400's, roughly from 1440 to 1500. One of the Paston letters (1453) ends, "The blessed Trinity have you in his keeping. Written at Norwich, on the Tuesday next after the conversion [of] St Paul"

(January 25); another (1449) ends, "[No] more I write to you at this time, but Holy Ghost have you in keeping. Written in haste, on St. Peter's Day by candlelight" (June 29). (The Pastons are not unusual in their habit of letter writing. Most of the upper classes in this century were surprisingly fluent writers.) In the will of Thomas Rotherham, Archbishop of York, a noble document, the date is set down as St. Bartholomew's Day.

Except in winter, the roads to English shrines—the palmers' ways—were crowded; and there were many shrines in England. Glastonbury—Avalon—where the holy thorn tree blossomed, was thirty miles or so from Bristol, in the West. At Pontefract, Yorkshire, was the tomb of Thomas, Earl of Lancaster, Edward II's cousin, beheaded in 1322, who, Froissart writes, "hath done many fair miracles at Pomfret." Lancastrians by going to his shrine showed their poor opinion of the Yorkist kings. In Gloucester Cathedral the murdered Edward II wrought miracles; and at the tomb of Henry VI, in the Abbey of Chertsey, fifteen miles up the Thames from London, "God wrought ... miracles ... for those of devout hearts." There were shrines at York and Lincoln in the North, St. Albans and Bury St. Edmunds near London, at Winchester, and at Wadham in the North (where there was "a cross of black marble miraculously found" in Saxon times). In Yorkshire was the cell of the Holy Rolle of Hampole, "neither monk nor doctor nor priest"; only an Oxford scholar, a hermit, a healer, a wanderer absorbed in God. There was, too, the shrine of St. Edward the Confessor in Westminster Abbey. And many lesser places were made sacred by less-known holy men and women, and by the minor saints. But no shrine could stand comparison with St. Thomas' at Canterbury or Our Lady of Walsingham's in Norfolk, one hundred ten miles north from London.

Pilgrims went on horseback, in horse litters (for great ladies, mainly, and the infirm and sick), and on foot—some barefoot, or the records say, "naked."

They went from different impulses, or by compulsion. Faith and earnestness—and custom—sent some. John Paston the Younger, in the heat of June and July, 1470, made pilgrimage on foot from Norfolk to Canterbury, one hundred seventy-five miles; and in September, 1471, "my Lord of Norfolk and my Lady were on pilgrimage to Our Lady on foot." Spring sent many out of doors into the sunshine and activity. For some the pilgrimage was a thanksgiving to God, or was the keeping of a vow—self-imposed or laid by the Church—to atone for sin and bring bright relief into a heavy life. The sick and infirm would see at Walsingham the sacred Image of Our Lady, and the Virgin's milk, and drink healing water and carry home the medals; and at Canterbury they saw the miraculous and splendid shrine of St. Thomas, and they could buy pewter ampullas, the small flasks stamped in Latin: *For the sick, Thomas is the best doctor.* They could fill these with holy water.

There were on the roads, mixed among the rest, minstrels and jugglers and acrobats, cheats and charletons, confidence men to prey upon the others, and murderers and "banned-men" and cutthroats to destroy. There were, too, those out for vacation, journeying sometimes happily all summer from one shrine to another. That is, the pilgrims were the usual run of people. None of them, probably, went on his pilgrimage from only one impulse. (Unless it was the cutthroats and those under penance or the very sick.) Most went because they felt like it. They wanted to go—a vague but most deciding cause. They, most of them, enjoyed the trip going and coming—the good inns and good companionship, the fairs, the sight of fine churches, the crowds and noise and vibrating high-colored movement which they saw on the way and in the towns. These they enjoyed along with (perhaps equally with) the Holy Image, the Masses and music, and their sense of lessened sin.

And the Church, though the pilgrims never at all realized it, was part of every breath and motion and feeling of the pilgrimage; was in every object and action—the dust of the road, the inn meals, the freeing moment before the altar.

Authorities favored the pilgrims. They kept up well the pilgrim roads; indeed, the fifteenth-century pilgrim roads were better than they were a hundred years later. They made the roads safe, too, so far as they could, against robbers and any mischance. And they tried to keep the costs of the journey within economy. In 1400 a pilgrim could hire a riding-horse from Southwark to Canterbury, about sixty-two miles, for twenty-four pence, with a change of horse at Rochester.

So the Church stood, a great, enfolding power—intimate and apart, of the earth and beyond it. It held as in a chalice the faith; and its way was largely the way of success here in the world. To a fifteenth-century man the Church was the ground under his feet; the earth he walked upon. It was the seen but unknown, beautiful sky—the heaven under which he breathed from his first breath to the last second in his life. And it was the constant air between earth and heaven. Quite literally, in his most wandering thoughts

7

or his most prosaic act, in spirit and body, in any height or depth, there was no time of his, no speech or language, where the voice of the Church was not heard. It presented the Sacrament; and, too, it blessed a fisherman's boat and in the country blessed the cattle and the fields and held Harvest Home.

The Church and the Nation

The conflict for authority between the State and the Papacy was complex, intricate in details, and immensely and constantly important; yet—by a wide sweep—it can be simplified to a struggle between the individuality of the English and the temporal claims of the World Church; between nationalism and feudalism; between King and Pope.

The conflict touched all classes (peasants, commons, lords, churchmen, royalty); all institutions (the family from birth to death, schools, guilds, the shires, the towns, the Court); all parts of the government—lawmaking and law administering; and people as unlike as Chaucer, Wycliffe, Wat Tyler, peasants and great landowners, Richard II, John of Gaunt, Rolle of Hampole, the Lord Chancellor Cardinal Wolsey. It was intimate in everyone's life.

Many in medieval England saw a way to end the division, but they saw different ways and a different end. For each one, his feelings and character and position and ability clouded and compounded the straight, bare, central question; as was natural. John of Gaunt and Wat Tyler never could have heard the same question asked, or have understood in the same way an answer, or a man.

The see-saw of tension between London and Rome had gone on since the Conquest. Henry II's penance for the murder of Becket, in 1172; King John's submission to Pope Gregory and his giving back England as a fief and paying feudal dues (the payment went on for one hundred twenty years) count as well-known gains of one side. An opposite swing shows in Henry II's claim to authority, and in John's signing the Magna Carta.

The 1400's inherited and extended the strong dispute. Back in 1305, for instance, laws were passed forbidding an appeal to any court outside England, or any implication that England was a feudal holding. In 1340 Edward III declared: "Know ye ... that our said realm of England, nor the people of the same of whatever estate or condition they be, shall not in any time to come be put in subjection nor obeisance" to power outside England. Ed-

8

ward III, holding to Wycliffe's logic, stopped for a time late in the century, the sending of Peter's Pence. And in 1380 Parliament forbade the giving of benefices "to divers people of another language, and of strange lands and nations, and sometimes to the utter enemy of the King and his realm."

Ten years later, a papal excommunication "cast out [the English] with the great curse, from the sight of Almighty God and the holy company of heaven . . . into everlasting damned company of hell." The Commons, again, were explicit. Since "the said things so attempted be clearly against the king's crown . . . the leige commons [declare they] will stand with our said lord the king . . . in the cases aforesaid, and in all other cases attempted against the king; in all points, to live and to die."

So, for centuries denials of temporal authority to the Church—less strong in their effect than in the wording—went on, until what had been protests and refusals became, in the 1500's, a revolution accomplished, the establishment of the separate Church, with the King as Head. England wanted to manage its own affairs temporal and spiritual: a typical English wish.

Through all the dispute the Church Eternal, of Christ's building, stood unquestioned: God's voice—the one guide into an eternity of joy.

* * * * *

Inside the nation even those who loved the Church brought sharp accusations against its servants. They were not any longer looking up for heavenly light or working to make England happier and better. They were lazy, rigid, corrupt.

The accusations had many forms, for many people sure of their judgments made them, but no one denied that the Church was his access to heaven. It was a constant presence. From birth to death it was the air he breathed, and his house, and his food. The True Church was sacred, as the Nation was; and so, whoever harmed it was to be rooted out and burned. Often, the cruelest acts were, to those doing them, the destruction of evil so that good might enter in.

Cleansing the body of the Church was part of the social struggle. In the two hundred years after 1250 (of which the 1400's were a large part) economic and class tension increased. It was especially strong from the Peasant's Revolt (1381) to Henry VIII's suppression of the monasteries (1536, 1539). Voices grew more sure in denouncing and in telling the remedy; and acts outside the law, more usual. Wat Tyler was sure enough of his purposes to put up his life for them. Rolle of Hampole, following his inward light, preached as remedy the perfectness of Christ's love. Wycliffe followed logic and Scriptures. Chaucer showed the England he saw—good and bad—in the *Canterbury Tales*. The Lord Chancellor Cardinal Wolsey had at heart full trust in his way to get success and in the value of that success.

In spite of laws and punishments the questions were fought over with cruel force. There were harsh and dreadful acts. The times were barbaric: a den of wolves. During a man's life, from 1399 to 1485, three English kings were murdered and one was killed in battle, and twelve princes of the blood and at least twelve other royal persons died violent deaths. Against his usual chivalry the Black Prince in 1370 burned Limoges and massacred three thousand citizens. Peasants in 1381 beheaded the Archbishop of Canterbury, the Lord Chief Justice, and the Lord Treasurer of England, and killed lawyers and landowners and foreign workmen. His own serfs in 1381 tortured the Prior of Bury St. Edmunds and at the end set up "his bloody head in the market place of his town." The Duke of Suffolk, next the King, had his head hacked off with six blows of a rusty sword. In June, 1450, Jack Cade's men dragged the Bishop of Salisbury "fro the autler and lad [him] up to an hille there . . . and they slew him horribly . . . and spoilled him unto the naked skin;" and they tore his bloody shirt into pieces to carry away. "In these times . . . the world being . . . at the mercy of a malignant whirlwind of fereful perturbations, which spread throughout nearly the whole of England, Satan again went forth."

Yet there was in the time pure and steady thinking, noble actions, saintliness, common sense, hard work, much business done well and government well carried on, and happy day-by-day routines. There were books, music, beautiful buildings, the ocean, good teaching and learning, great pleasures in what can be done in this world and some thoughts about the next, meditations by a few on the perfection of Christ's love; and for most, most of the time, the inescapable, bearable cares and sorrow and suffering. Everywhere were good fathers and mothers, and good children. So —as is common— the King was in his countinghouse, the Queen in her parlor, Simple Simon went to the Fair, and Humpty-Dumpty had just fallen from his wall again.

Four Voices

Out of the confusion and contradictions of the century, there are voices which give answer. Some imply by the whole substance of what they say; some make a formal prescription. Each one, speaking, follows his own way, sure, it seems, of his road and his end.

Among them were Rolle of Hampole, Wat Tyler, Wycliffe, and Chaucer. They were very different from each other. Their minds and spirits, and their aims and actions and talk, and even the kind of words they said make direct contradictions. Yet each was part of the time. He spoke out of it and for it. Each had strong effect on the 1400's, and so, on the next century and the centuries that followed.

Rolle of Hampole

Richard Rolle of Hampole, a scholar and dreamer ("the greatest of English mystics"), at eighteen gave up his study at Oxford and the usual, institutional practices of the Church, and a wanderer absorbed in God, meditating "the sweetness of Christ's love," preached and wrote and healed. His great wish was that everyone should share "joy in the life of Jesus." Then happiness would be in everyone, and all things on earth and hereafter would be right.

He wrote a good deal in Latin and English. His writings affirm his personal, eager, springing certainties—those of a spirit centered in the good which might come and not at all in denials, changes, and destroying. He hoped to draw others to the truth by opening to them its lovely certainty. He does not argue, or advocate social and ethical reforms. Each man, by himself and within his own spirit—though "full far from the sweetness of Christ's love"—can of himself draw near and follow and be clean.

Three sentences—verses—from his *Epistle III* show his way and his desires:

> Wash thy thoughts clean with tears of love, and with burning desire that He shall find nothing foul in thee, for His joy is that thou be fair and lovely in His eyes. Loveliness of soul, which Christ desires from thee, is that thou be pure and meek, gentle, bearing and enduring wickedness. And set thy heart upon the memory of his passion and his wounds: great joy and sweetness shalt thou feel if thou wilt contemplate the pains Christ suffered for thee.

He tells this of his awakening:

> I was sitting for sooth in a chapel [He was then at Oxford, a very young man], and while I was delighting in the sweetness of prayer and meditation, suddenly I felt a merry and unknown heat in me. At first I was uncertain, doubting from whom it could be. After a long

time I became convinced it was not of a creature but of my Maker. . . . Whilst truly I sat in the same chapel. . .praying to heaven with all desire, suddenly, in what manner I know not, I felt in me the noise of song and was aware of the most pleasing, heavenly melody. . .a continual mirth of sound. [and] for fullness of inward delight I burst out, then, singing the love of God. . . .

His central certainty was close to this:

> Good it is to be a preacher; but better. . .and sweeter to be a contemplator, to have a foretaste of eternal bliss, to sing the delights of Eternal Love.

What he has written is very real and strange and individual. Clearly, he felt direct communion with God. He walked by a light not of this world, and saw by what Sir Thomas Browne called "the invisible sun within us."

The Peasants' Revolt

In 1348 and 1349 the Black Death killed close to one-third of the people of England. It had come out of Asia, spread through Europe along the trade-routes of Italy, Flanders, and Spain, and entered England in the late summer; foretold by "a dreadful comet," rains that were blood, and monsters of sea and air and land. Even in the protection of the King's household, high Court officers died from it. No isolated country house or hidden village was safe. In many towns the plague, or fear of the plague, left churches, law courts, business exchanges, and whole streets empty of people. Land and sea traffic slowed to almost nothing. Not enough men were left to work the fields.

When the plague was almost ended, laws were passed that every man must work, and at the wages common before the plague. To hold in place the common laborer, "puffed up and quarrelsome," the laws laid penalties both on those who would not work and on landlords who over-paid by "flesh, fish, or food." Against these Statutes of Laborers, landowners and landworkers were strongly set. The new laws were defied. "Divers persons of small incomes . . . laborers" joined into companies which would work only on their own terms. They did "gather themselves in great routs and agree by such confederacy that everyone shall aid other to resist their lord with strong hands—Lords of Manors as well as men of Holy Church. [They] do menace . . . their lords of life and members."

Through the next thirty years, the nation—laborers, employers, and lawmakers—went ahead, baffled and restless and increasingly unhappy under the tension of rising prices, heavy taxation, and the steady drain of the French War. In 1377 a boy of ten and a half—Richard II—became king; and a child as king was wholly new in England.

The unrest grew. In 1379 a fresh income tax "caused great distress and woe." It touched everyone. A duke paid £6 13s. 4d.; a laborer, 4d. The next year a poll tax of three groats was imposed: 12d. "Twelve pence was pay for two weeks' work at haying time." It was to be paid, the act read, by "every person in the kingdom, male or female, of an age of fifteen, of what rank and condition so ever except beggars." The country paid the tax; but with "great grudging and many a bitter curse." Steadily, in the thirty years after the Black Plague the cost of food, rent, and clothing increased.

By the spring of 1381 a resistance had risen to armed revolt. Taxation was not the cause of revolt, but it sharpened into action the anger held against the government and the clergy, and the long-felt hatred for bad landlords. All over England uprisings came, spontaneous ones it seemed. The center was the southeast counties—Kent, Essex, Suffolk, all close to London. There, by the first of June, writes Professor Froude, repeating the ancient account, "a hundred thousand men" were in arms, an incredible number for a population of not more than two million people. But the exaggeration may gauge the general fear. Probably, at the end, fifty thousand men camped near London.

Their leaders were Wat Tyler and John Ball. Different verdicts have been passed on Tyler. His own time (but all from the classes which were against him) said he was "a quick-witted, ambitious, self-reliant fellow, with an insolent tongue"; "a well-known rogue and robber"—le plus grand larron et robbare (1381); "one of the most notorious highwaymen and thieves of the country" (1381); "a traitor" (1381). After his time, he has been judged: "an obscure adventurer of ready wit and sharp tongue" (1864); "mob leader [with no] definite scheme for the . . . governance of England" (1916); "one of the great figures, the symbols of freedom [who] stand for the inarticulate commons" (1954?); "a shadow" (1940); "an adventurous opportunist . . . thrown out of the whirlpool of events" (1955).

John Ball was much older than Tyler. He seems, fairly looked at, to have been an illiterate, wandering priest—a "hedge-parson," excommunicated fourteen years before the outbreak. To those of authority in his time he was "the mad priest of Kent"; one "be-

13

guiling the ears of the laity by invectives, and putting about scandals concerning [the Church], dreadful language such as shocks the ears of Christians" (1380); one who went "preaching social equality, and schisms, and scandals against just men." He was in prison for such talk when the Revolt began.

Both men are only wavering, unoutlined figures in history; no great matter since the action of the Revolt and its aims seem clear. It aimed at a few specific, economic changes; it had no large plan beyond the changes; its way was force. The "simple politics" of the peasants was loyalty to King Richard; death to his evil councillors; and so, a new world for the poor.

Tuesday, June 12, the peasants—whom Wat Tyler kept under surprising discipline when he wished—came to Southwark. That day, they broke into the Cathedral during Mass, burned two prisons, and looted and burned the palace of the Archbishop and many houses and shops. Then they stood, a little time, looking across the Thames at London. Next day, Wednesday the thirteenth, they poured over London Bridge into the city. "Tumultuous in the extreme," they broke open and burned more prisons; burned John of Gaunt's Palace of the Savoy, west of the Temple, "the most magnificent belonging to any subject in the land"; burned the Temple, where they killed all the lawyers they could lay hands on, (Lawyers made laws); and butchered about four hundred Flemish workmen. (They were not English.)

Thursday, June 14, in good discipline, they marched to "the Meadow of Mile End," two and a half miles east of London beyond the walls, a pleasant open plain. King Richard rode to meet them. He was fourteen and a half years old, "forward and intelligent," tall, handsome, golden-haired, popular then with his people, the son of their great Black Prince. The peasants faced him with four demands: no slavery, lowering of land rent to fourpence an acre—a usual rent; liberty to buy and sell goods and their labor at any market or fair; and pardon for the past.

These the King agreed to; and he gave them a royal banner; and he kept his clerks up all night writing charters to be sent every parish and township in England. A good part of the peasants —that is, most of the "honest and simple folks"—accepted the King's word, and so went back home. Wat Tyler, who seems to have wanted no agreement, broke into the Tower with four hundred men (probably the same day), murdered the Archbishop of Canterbury Simon of Sudbury, and "frightened into a faint" Joan, the King's mother. But he let her go safely into the city.

Wat Tyler made new, and hindering, demands. On the fifteenth the King ("after taking the sacrament and making confession as in time of danger") and his retinue rode out to meet him and the peasants still with him. This time they met at Smithfield, a housed-in market-square by the church of St. Bartholomew, just outside the northwest angle of the City wall. There Wat Tyler was stabbed, his men were scattered, pardons were revoked, and the Revolt came to its end in uproar and punishments and death, and in a continuing but hidden resistance. Wat Tyler's head, they put up on London Bridge. At Bury St. Edmunds John Ball was hanged and drawn and quartered, and his head was set high in the market-place—as the Prior's head had been—close by the great Priory the Revolt had burned.

The Revolt was not straight out against the Church, but it was against landlords, and the Church was a great landlord. It was against taxes and restrictions, and so, with primitive direct-ness, was against those who made the laws. Many churchmen were among the lawmakers. The peasants beheaded the Archbishop of Canterbury and burned his Palace of Lambeth because he was Lord Chancellor, as they had burned the palace of the King's uncle, John of Gaunt, and would have killed him if they had found him. He was to them a very wicked and powerful man, the King's enemy and theirs. Just then, in early June, he was on the Border fighting the Scots. The Peasants' Revolt in the North was so strong that his life was in danger, but no English town would open its gates to him, for his safety. To save himself, he made a truce with the Scots and then "withdrew to Edinboro, where he was well en-tertained."

The Revolt passed a verdict on the Church or rather on church-men. The sanctity of his office did not put a churchman who was part of the government above the people's judgment and ven-geance. In the 1300's most officers of government were churchmen. Two-thirds of the English and Welsh bishops were in the service of Edward III or of his sons. The Revolt made clear, too, that many in England thought that physical force was an honest, direct, strong, sure way to bring reform. Force would be used even against the Church.

Through three days Wat Tyler seems to have had England at his mercy; but he had no plan beyond one day for the future of England, or for his own.

He and the peasants in revolt did not have logic as Wycliffe had; or one illuminating light, like Rolle's; or, like Chaucer, wis-

15

dom and culture and experience. Their thinking was clumsy, incomplete, formless, bewildered: in one view, pitiful. They turned to violence with a primitive and frightful certainty. But they were one voice of the time.

John Wycliffe (1320-1384)

Until he was forty-five, Wycliffe was an academic philosopher; his study was theology; his method was the dialectics of the schoolmen. The year of the Black Death (1348) he was twenty-eight, and he lived three years after the Peasants' Revolt.

In the first two-thirds of his life he was a student and a teacher at Oxford and the master of Balliol College; the vicar of a parish, a royal chaplain, a learned man who stood well at Court; and a writer and preacher. Then, in the last twenty years, he turned to matters of the Church: what inherently was its part on earth, how well did it carry that out, and what was its relation to the State. This led him into social inquiry and much writing for the King against papal claims; into translating the Bible; and into sending out his missionaries—"Wycliffe's heretical missionaries" to some: the Poor Priests, the young men not ordained or bound by vows, who in russet gowns, with pilgrim's staff and wallet, barefoot, went about preaching on village commons, in church-yards, at fairs and cross-roads and anywhere else that men came. Twice in the last ten years of his life (1376, 1378) he was tried in London for heresy and condemned, but in the end he was "given only a gentle admonition." In 1382 he was expelled from his Oxford teaching. Forty-four years after his death his body was burned as a heretic's, and the ashes were scattered on the river Swift.

The center of Wycliffe's belief was that each person should make his own decisions "on the basis of Scripture and reason," and should carry them out. Each should examine for himself a civil law or a practice of the Church (say, the Eucharist), weigh it for truth, and follow his judgment. "As we are damned each one alone, so are we saved alone." The Bible, he accepted literally. Mind and conscience, he entirely trusted. All truth rested in the *lex Christi—* the divine law.

Humanly (leaving unsettled the power of everyone to reason out truth), it was a narrow doctrine, for it denied emotion. The doctrine in its extreme held that Litany, music, Latin, statues and stained glass and paintings, great buildings, all forms and displays shut away the truth. They came between; they biased judgment, as an intense memory might, or some strong association. To Chau-

16

cer, who was a poet, truth was a unity of fact and feeling and expression. Light came by its embodiment, or rather the light and the embodiment were one.

Though wise in his ideas, Wycliffe was sometimes so intent on thinking them to their limits that his extremes were beyond possible practice. They were grotesques. His climbing logic brought him out on remote icy peaks, from which he had to climb down and find the way home. It is easy to write against his extremes of logic, which now and then identified themselves as reductions to absurdity and were quite against the English habit of adjustment and sensible compromise. If they had been followed, few matters of Church and State would have stood. Fortunately, Wycliffe—home again—knew which of his ideas were only acrobatic exercises.

Wycliffe can show a curiously flat landscape. His nature (and, steadily, his occupations and acts) isolated him from strong human emotion, good or bad. He had no traffic with the world of Chaucer or of Rolle of Hampole. Equally, he was separate from users of physical force, the fighters and quarrelers, and from the politicians —in the Church and at Court—who were satisfied to do what could be done then and there—as the times went and people being what people were and no nonsense talked.

Wycliffe lived for forty years at Oxford and among his parishioners at Luttleworth, and was all his life among many fairly usual men and women and the few unusual. But there is no record of his close friendship with anyone. Today, those writing of him do not break into sudden applause. They write the words *logic, Christian democracy, economic views, opinions,* and *tenets* and *theory.* They use the words of philosophy. They do not write of his sympathy or compassion or insight; and no one has ever written of his humor.

But his limits of mind and temperament do not in the end count much beside what he did. He saw that the Bible was translated. He defended England against feudal claims. He preached that every man's duty was to think and to decide for himself, and to act justly. He had courage, integrity, strength of thought; was no self-seeker; and his tenacity in what he had found true held out against the world. All his life, he was concerned about important matters—not satisfied with watching the flickering shapes and colors of what was trivial. He was highly gifted and highly trained; a practical and hard-working man. At Oxford, for forty years he was a light and a flame. He seems never to have believed physical force settled a social or moral question. And because the spirit of God was in each man, he honored men—at Court, in the parish, at

Oxford, and (by his Poor Priests) in the villages and cross-roads of the shires. That is, he treated people as intelligent and honest and responsible. He had faults enough to save him to humanity. These abstractions are made clearer by seeing his part in questions of the Church and of the State.

He was sure the Church had gone away from the people. Though many of the clergy were saintly, learned, brave, constant in their work, yet the Church as a whole was selfish and unfaithful. It had not risen and perfected its ways and brought its life into the lives of the people, for their good.

The Church was rigid. It had not changed. Other institutions were changing. The guilds were, and the wool trade and all other commerce, and the schools. In war, cannons and long-bows were coming to be used. Buildings were gaining a new kind of beauty. The English had begun even to make their own bricks, and to put in fireplaces for comfort, and wider windows with clearer glass set into them. Italy and Asia were closer; the motions of the planets were more clearly seen; the mists over the Atlantic were thinning.

But through it all the Church still held the old ways. It spent its energy on matters not of the spirit. At its best it gave a smoky light. Bishops should not be men of the world. They should not, for one thing, hold high government offices. (From 1378 to 1388, of the twenty-five bishops in England and Wales, twenty-one or so were in the service of the King or his sons.) A good churchman "dwelleth at hoom and kepte wel his folde." The Church should not lay up treasures on earth. (By 1500 it held one-third of the wealth of England.) Though no churchman should live a worldly life, yet he should not shut himself away from others. He should work in the open air of his time yet keep his thoughts and actions beyond the temporal. Much else was wrong. For surely the Church ought to show an image, though imperfect, of the Church Eternal; not hold out to its people false doctrines and idle forms, and sell for money what could be won only through the spirit. The fields of the Church indeed lay barren; its springs were tainted; the waters, muddy. He did not, for it was not his nature, tell the Church it had no passion of love and faith and did not trust earnestly day and night in God, and did not glow with ardor for the souls of men.

Some verses in *Piers Plowman*, though written as satire, show one usual belief of the time:

Clerks that are tonsured should neither toil nor sweat nor work...
...heirs of heaven [are] all that are tonsured...
Prayers of perfect men...[are] the dearest labor that pleaseth our Lord.

18

With all this, Wycliffe disagreed absolutely. Yet many saw great good in the cloistered life, which Wycliffe judged empty, and worse.

Wycliffe had positive belief about the relations of England with the Papacy. Clearly, England never could be a feudal state. It was sovereign; itself of itself. It might have a Church common to other nations (as it had a common air and ocean, or common trade-routes), but the nation was its sole self; a unity, one realm against the four corners of the earth. Wycliffe gave Edward III a logical and legal basis for refusing the feudal claim of the Papacy, the first reasoned defense an English king had had. His logic was: The Papacy was a spiritual dominion; No spiritual dominion could hold temporal power; So the Papacy could not demand feudal service, or anything else. Wycliffe added that a gift to the Church was charity—a gift which came by grace of the giver and not by the right of the one who received. Neither King John nor the Lords and Commons could put England into the rule of the Pope.

And, too, beyond even logic stood the first law of a nation—self-preservation. To give homage to any power, to pay it a tribute of money, to set alien citizens in offices was treason to the king and heresy before God. For a nation, like a person, was bound to protect its life.

In 1300 less than half the people of England were freemen. A serf could not plead in a court against his lord, or sell his labor, or leave his land without his lord's permission. All through the century, serfs and those bound by service to the land, and the tenants of bad landlords were moving, bewildered and bitter, into an open revolt. The naked were crying out to the king. Wycliffe wrote of this:

> Strife, contests, and debates ben used in our land, for lords striven with their tenants to bring them in thraldom...Also lords many times do wrongs to poor men by extortions, and unreasonable... taxes, and take poor men's goods and payen not therefore...and menace and sometimes beat them when they ask their pay. And thus lords devour poor men's food...and they perish for mischief and hunger and thirst and cold, and their children also.

He was sure an evil man had no right to property. He reasoned that since God was Infinite Goodness, He could give no possessions to the evil man, and, therefore, the evil landlord was landless. Yet by his equal logic Wycliffe was sure of the contrary.

> The fiend moveth some men to say that Christian men should not be servants or thralls to heathen lords...[But no] servants or tenants may lawfully withhold rents or services from their lords, when lords ben

openly wicked in their living...[Though] in a manner they eat and drink poor men's flesh and blood, and ben manquellers [man-killers] ...God permitteth them to hold.

The union between the contradictions was the word *hold*. God permitted men to *hold*, but He did not give them *possession*. Wycliffe's sincere distinction between *usus* (hold) and *dominium* (possession) is his philosopher's way out from the contradiction. In the long run his unification—his compromise—worked better than either violent extreme could have. Wycliffe's logic found a center of usable, lasting good sense.

Wycliffe is a great man. He did have much that limited him. He was not a humanist or a poet or a saint (though he could have been a martyr); not a balanced, wide, benign philosopher; not a companion for every day and all day. And we may prefer silence, or the fresh quiet of rain, to his pressing logic. But he is a very great man in what he was, and in what he is today. That is clear at the end of even a surface study of him.

If he blurred a main truth by his schoolman's energy after its extremes, in time he came back to the wisdom of the center. He kept the main track, even if by dialectics and forgetting and contradiction. Something in him was stronger even than his pursuit of his divine philosophy. But he did enjoy the pursuit of an idea, the excitement (rather, in him the mental satisfaction) of keeping the ball in the air as long as he could.

Geoffrey Chaucer

Yes, I knew Blake well, and liked him, and respected him...There never was an honester man than he, or one who lived in finer poverty, —poor but strictly simple in his habits. I remember his wife, who was a very nice good woman, once said to me, '*Oh I have very little of Mr. Blake's company, he passes all his life in Paradise*'—Seymour Kirkup to Charles Eliot Norton, Florence, 1870; Norton *Letters*, I, 373-377.

Chaucer lived on earth. He had many occupations there. He was a poet, a businessman who worked hard, a gentleman used to the Court, the King's ambassador in Italy and France, always a reader (his *Cicero,* he said, was an "olde boke totoren"), a learned humanist, and a city man who loved the country.

He was not earth-bound. He had clear judgments; strong abstract ethics of action and feeling. The *Canterbury Tales* shows he had thought about the small hour-by-hour puzzles, and about love, the Church, poetry, business, learning, London and the fields outside, people, and about what was the good and evil in life. Because he was a poet, he did not carry on his search by syllogisms and give its end in an abstraction. He showed the search and the end by showing people or telling a story. He told of the Knight, the Poor Parson, the Wife of Bath, the Somonour, the Cook, Griselda, Chanticleer, and his telling has wisdom, charm, reality, humor, and action.

He liked people and he saw what they were. He saw their faces, and their nature, and the color and cut of their clothes, and heard their voices—lisping or gentle or superior or solemn, or young like the Squire's or rich like the Host's.

He was not hard on most of those he lived among. He gave homage to nobility of spirit, but he was tolerant of imperfection—except of what was mean, ungenerous, vicious, wholly self-pleased. He was delighted by the gusto of the men and women around him and in his imagination; by the healthy, crude pleasure they got out of life. He was a happy man, quite healthy himself in spirit and feeling. So one guesses. He was a friendly man. At any rate the *Canterbury Tales* read aloud seem direct and personal talk.

Chaucer—so intelligent, so experienced, so definite (though tolerant) in ideas and tastes, so great a poet—gave his judgments of the time. They are quite unlike Rolle's, Wat Tyler's, or Wycliffe's. He was no mystic: he would never have seen a seraph filling the whole sky, as St. Francis did. He was sure that physical force was not the way to an ideal. And he could not trust schoolmen's logic, or any logic alone, to find reality.

About England and the Papacy he wrote nothing. He does imply a great deal by his steadily-shown belief in nationalism and his pleasure in the very English traits of the Knight, the Poor Parson, the Wife of Bath, and other persons in the *Prologue* whom he likes. Though he lived during the Peasants' Revolt, he wrote only once of it—three lines, with no opinion given. Of the Church he saw about him in England he wrote constantly. He was a son of the Church, not like Wycliffe half-in, half-out of it; but he saw its grave faults.

The fifty-two lines in which he wrote of the Poor Parson have in them the substance of his whole opinion of the Church; and two lines of it are his lasting text:

...rich he was of holy thought and work.
He was also a learned man, a clerk.

The "also" tells Chaucer's value of learning—splendid to want and to have, but infinitely less than goodness.

2

TOWNS

People of the 1400's breathed the air of their century. They ate what the century set on the table; they dressed as it prescribed; slept at hours accepted by their time; and often thought the round, easy ideas of their day. That is, they followed the fashion. They pronounced their words, made war and traded and sang, taught their children, farmed, governed the kingdom, built their towns, and believed or disbelieved very much in accepted ways. Even when they dissented, the present was the point of separation, and the present earth was the first they wanted to change.

Yet it was the people themselves who had made these forms; and the forms, which seem to rule, explain and express their makers.

To see any part of what was physically around the people of the fifteenth century, and, besides, to surmise from it what they had in the invisible and hidden world of their minds, bring from two sources a gain in reality.

London and other towns gave back one image of this reality.

The Spirit and the Shapes

English towns of the 1400's were democratic in spirit, and their democracy was strong and articulate, especially in the largest towns —London, York, Norwich, Chester, Bristol. If English towns did not always agree in opinion, they did agree in purpose. London had about fifty thousand people (by 1500 it might have had seventy thousand); York, twelve thousand; the three others, each ten thousand or less. In these towns and others the citizens made the public opinion, carried on the actions, and held offices—usually without pay. Robert Rede of York, about 1450, when the Earl of

Northumberland tried to name the mayor, said, "The mayor must be chosen by the commonalty, and not by no lord"; and he was so chosen. Every town was jealous of its civic rights and its place in the nation, and each citizen was aggressively alert about his rights in the town. Such local unity and personal claim gave a town its power in the nation and its vigor within itself. All of them seem to have had this unity; and the center for agreement, the main purpose in all the towns, seems to have held constant in spite of the great differences among citizens in wealth, position and authority, occupation, interests, education, and even in birth. This steady purpose was the good of the town, of the whole body: high clerics, nobles, great merchants, guildsmen, common workers, and even the dregs—paupers, lepers, criminals—the accumulating and inevitable refuse of the town.

The government was democratic, though not all townsmen had part in it. A town was centered in its middle class—the majority and the governing power. Indeed, the middle class (a very inclusive term) *was* the town—an overstatement with truth in it. Town government was organized (much as, in form, London's is today) around the twelve great Merchant Companies—mercers', drapers', grocers', fishmongers', goldsmiths', and the others; and the prime purpose of magistrates and courts and guilds was to assure each citizen safety and reasonable comforts.

London showed most clearly the life and the anatomy of a medieval English town. But London only magnified the aims and organization—spirit and body—of, say, Stratford-on-Avon or Hull or York—the second city. Courts and elected officials stood up for law and for each citizen's rights. Their oversight ranged from food supply and water supply and fuel and trading by land and river and ocean (the main matters); through health and sanitation (rather unsolved, these, for London and the rest had no covered sewers and few house drains); into the price and quality of anything a tradesman sold, and civic pageantry and music and festivals.

So the town kept its oversight of great local matters and looked after, equally, the smallest detail. Because he had sold "corrupt wine . . . not good or wholesome for mankind," a City court in the 1400's ruled that "John Penrose should drink a draught of the same wine which he sold to the common people; and the remainder of such wine shall be poured on the head of the same John; and that he shall forswear the calling of a vintner in the city of London for ever," unless he gained the king's pardon. John Russell, who had "exposed 37 pigeons for sale, putrid, rotton, stinking and abominable to the human race," is to be in "the pillory, and the said pigeons are to be burnt beneath the pillory, and the cause of his punishment to be proclaimed." The court of trial wrote that he had done this evil "to the scandal, contempt, and disgrace of all the City"—against, that is, its spirit, intent, and law.

London and other towns—but London most—had constant and critical interest in national affairs and had great power in them; because, if a town liked, it could raise a good number of troops and its merchants could make the loans needed for any war. The towns kept their independence of judgment, and watched to protect their liberties and their trade. They were, too, quite ready to tell positively what were their rights and their powers. London sided in strength as it pleased and where its sympathy and interests were: with Henry VI against Edward IV, or with Richard III, or with Henry VII. All the York and Lancastrian kings found that out.

It was contradictory but natural that, though the towns stood together in aim and government, they did stand vigorously apart. They never, it is true, were enemies to one another as towns in Italy or Germany might be, or steadily set spear points against the king as in fifteenth-century Spain. They were not feudal holdings, or so weak that they had no influence. A town was one strong expression of common English energy and spirit. Still, each had its personality and its habits; the colors of its opinions and emotions; its local history and local interests and prejudices; its loyalties and festivals and foods and saints and physical surroundings—the special, divergent flow of its life. London, York, Bristol, and Norwich —south, north, west, east—were far from each other and from Stratford and Chester and Rye. Each built its houses from differing stuff; from limestone, wood, plaster, brick, flint. They said their words differently, and locally held to different trades, had around them moors or rich midland fields or fen country, or the Thames, the Ouse River, the sea. Within its close and intimate world each town held its own people and ways, the land it knew, its limiting and familiar horizon.

Yet this individuality was, most of it, specialization of what all the towns had in common; variations on a theme—variations strongly sounded, theme often submerged. The differences can seem strong; much depends on what one wants to see. For the towns did get along with each other. They were at home with one another. They had, it is important to realize, the same language and history and church and government; were largely the same race;

and had much the same ways of thinking and being educated and getting a living. They had the same riddles to answer. They liked (with reservations) each other's sports and festivals and music; and it is fair even to say that they lived with the same sky and fields and ocean. Wood, stone, or brick, their buildings were English, not built for Italy or Flanders. The land and water around any of them was in England; not in Normandy or Castile. A northern moor was English, and so—definitely—were the Avon and the Thames. The burr of Somerset talk and the long, flattened vowels of Yorkshire—strange to a Londoner—were English speech, the mother tongue.

All the towns were busy looking after much the same matters. For example, waterways (the Thames, the Ouse at York, the Atlantic, the ocean routes to Spain, the North Sea) were crowding concerns to London and York and Bristol and Norwich. York through most of the 1400's was struggling to keep the Ouse, its way to the ocean, free of the obstructing fish-traps (*fishgarths*; dams, nets, "wicker rooms to trap . . . salmon") which great land-owning nobles and clergy built in the river to catch fish for their tables. London had its eyes on the commerce that came up the Thames in foreign ships, and on its coastal trade. Norwich, for at least a century, kept at making safe its wool trade across the North Sea. Bristol watched its great ocean to the south and west.

"Gay go up And gay go down. . . ."

OLD LONDON RHYME

A medieval town was a noisy place in the crowded business wards. In these the streets were narrow (often a dozen feet wide or less), stone-paved, closed in by the high-walled, overhanging fronts of buildings five or six storeys tall—good sounding boards. Opposite roof tops almost touched. The shops—stalls, really—were small and very many, and were so narrow that fifteen crowded into one hundred fifty feet along Cheapside, west of Old Jewry. There were no sidewalks; the pavement sloped from the crown, the high center, to the kennels, where mud and filth lay or ran. Along the streets, over the cobbles or flat stones or earth, went springless carts, men on horseback, horse-borne litters, the pushing crowd. In the street mixed the cries and countercries of wandering street-sellers and of apprentices before the open-fronted shops; the beating out of iron upon a blacksmith's anvil, hammering of carpenters, pounding on sheet copper from a kettlemaker's; the hubbub and swirl of a sudden street fight. And, typical of many others like him, a cook at the door of his eating place (so *Piers Plowman* says) was bawling, "Hot pies, hot! Good [pies of pork] and of geese! Come, eat! Come!" Besides, people might be singing; and all day church-bells rang. There were one hundred sixty churches in London.

The Londoners, then and later, liked their bells. Bow Bells, they were sure, had talked sensibly to Dick Whittington in the early 1400's. With affectionate familiarity they made up rhymes that gave to each chime its personality and its own talk. "'Oranges and lemons,' Say the bells of St. Clements." (St. Clements Danes still gives to the children, on a Sunday in March, the oranges and lemons the bells have "said.") Queen Elizabeth, it is told, "as a girl . . . would pause and listen with attention, and commend the bells"; and when she was queen she showed gratitude to the bells which had rung at her release from the Tower, when she was nineteen. The east window of St. Olave's Hart Street pictures her, in stained glass, standing royally dressed with two tall bells at her side. And in 1660, one evening when Samuel Pepys went home through London, happy that Charles II had come back at last to England, "the bells rang everywhere."

People enjoyed the streets. When the weather was possible, they were out of doors to look and talk and be alive. May Day, the opening out into spring, was a happy time. On Easter morning the sun danced as it rose. Sunshine was best, but in the street at any time was diversion and companionship and business. "One could have thought there was always a fair in this town," an old chronicle said. A central street was a mirror of life, *speculum vitae,* with motion and sound and sharp color added. Color was all about. Some house-fronts were carved and sharply painted and gilded, some were washed white or pink, some were solid black and white; horses went by, gay with trappings; people—every sort of English and foreigner—were kaleidoscopic; even shoes were green and red. A procession was a rainbow, with wide space in its spectrum for orange and indigo and red. The Thames, London's greatest highway, showed its special pageantry. A street was a new, living, illuminated book; and there were not many other books for reading. Besides, a house was apt to be crowded, airless, ill-lit. Many were tall tenements—a family on each floor. And, too, privacy, inside a house or outside, was not yet much valued by anyone, or even much imagined.

Such streets held a stridency of mingled sounds, higher in pitch and more sharply punctuated than the heavily pulsing, mechanic noise of our city streets. The large towns knew their own uproar and—a little troubled by it—made ordinances to lessen it or to confine it to set times and districts. Some forbade any "Knockking fyling [and other] noysefulle werke" before five o'clock on a summer morning and daylight in winter. All the year, most work waited for the sun. The towns kept in mind this need for restraint. To each town it was a part, though a small part, of the town's main purpose, which in the ultimate was to build "a fair and lasting city."

To a degree hard to realize now towns were the center of trading. A village, even a small one, was likely to have, besides cottages, a manor house, a church, probably a tythe barn and perhaps a school, but no shops or home-selling places at all. Country people —that meant the village people, since everyone outside a town lived near the common lands, and not on isolated farms—got from their fields most that they ate and wore and used; or they had it by trade from a neighbor or gift of the manor; or they bought it at local fairs. They bought, too, from chapmen and wandering tinkers—part peddlers, part montebanks, part newsmen—who carried to the villages goods and gossip, ballads and broadsides and news and jokes and general enlivening, along with pots and pans, ribbons, salt, cloth, scissors and knives and needles, and much more such foreign stuff.

Retail trade was, of course, active in the towns. It usually was much divided. To get, say, a cushion might mean buying the cloth at one shop, feathers at another, and fringe and whatever made the rest of it, at some other. In these large towns this specialization usually was less; yet even in them it was strong.

In the century a trade often kept to one part of town or to one street. All through the life of the time this union of like with like shows up strongly and in unexpected relations. It was a firm-set English quality, which made a unity of the family, of those in one community, or of those in one business or profession or rank. It even kept a trade to its own part of town.

Some London wards got their names from such association. The brewers lived in Vintry Ward, central London, "near to the friendly water of Thames," which carried their ships. Cordwainers were in Cordwainer Ward. Lime Street Ward "taketh the name [from] making or selling of lime there (as is supposed)." But the names of many wards came out of the kind of country they once had been. Through Langborne Ward once had flowed "a long bourne [brook; Scotch, burn] of sweet water, which of old time breaking . . . into small shares, rills, or streams . . . ran south to the river Thames."

Fennie About—a pleasant, puzzling name for that ward—shows it might once have been "a fenny or moorish ground," or it might have been where hay was sold. Grass Street was close by.

Streets were named from this centering of business. Italians lived in Lombard Street. Hart Street by the Tower had been a place for buying hearthstones. The Poultry (Cheapside near the Mansion House), Haymarket, Ironmonger Lane, Hosier Lane by St. Bartholomew's Hospital, and Milk Street explain themselves. The meaning of some place names has been hidden by time; for a word may change the color of its light with time, and from other words the meaning may fade out altogether. Cordwainer Ward— the leatherworkers'—got the name because Cordova in Spain made much fine leather; in Cheapside all kinds of trading went on, and *ceap* is Anglo-Saxon for *trade*. Fetter Lane—Holburn to Fleet—is said to be named from the *faitours,* the beggars, once there; and of course at Cornhill, now crowded in the City, "Time out of mind, a corn market was holden." The *wick* in Candlewick Street (the place "for candles, both wax and tallow") means *maker, wright.* Panyer Alley, in the City, was once given up to the basketmakers. Bowyers' Row made bows for shooting. Pater Noster Row made beads—rosary beads. Pattens' Lane had made pattens—the clogs much used then: the wooden soles with cleats crosswise on the bottom, worn to raise shoes above water and the general street-muck. Garlickhithe, on the Thames, was very much less a market place for the gross garlic than it was for the aromatic, legendary, winged spices of the East. Bread Street was "so called of bread in old tyme sold there," but Pye Corner—where Falstaff went in II Henry IV—never had been given over to pastry.

Memorials

> ...the memorials and the things of fame
> That do renown this city...
>
> TWELFTH NIGHT

Unto the noble, ancient, and renowned city, the city of London, in England, I William Caxton, citizen...of the same, and of the fraternity and fellowship of the mercers...owe of right my service and good will, and of very duty am bound naturally to assist, aid, and counsel as farforth as I can to my power as to my mother, of whom I have received my nourishing and living. And [I] shall pray for the good prosperity of the same during my life.—Caxton, *Book Called Caton,* 1483.

Caxton, a Londoner, and until he was fifty an official in the Mercers' Company, dedicated *Cato* to the City of London. His gift, "this smal lytyl booke [which] conteyned a short and prouffitable doctryne for al maner of peple," he wrote and published ten years after he set up his press in Westminster. It is a series of homilies, with curious attending anecdotes. His purpose in writing just this kind of book is interesting, if aside. The book, he hoped, would draw young people to struggle for the good of London (for the "comyn wele") and for the "right gouernaunce of their body and sowle." To both these the young were less attentive than they had been when he was a boy, fifty years before. Perhaps the date of the book—the first, uneasy year of Richard III's reign—may show some cause for his anxiety.

Caxton was one in the multitude who gave. Those who gave usually made material gifts—schools, hospitals and almshouses, churches, markets, exchanges, guildhalls, reservoirs and fountains and conduits for water, libraries, and other such visible expressions of their gratitude. The name of a donor was sometimes recorded—written or carved—in the vestry of his parish church. "It passeth my power," wrote Froissart, "to compile the Benefactors, Natives of the City, whose names in *fair Tables* (the Counterpart of the Original, no doubt kept in Heaven) [stand] in their respective Parishes; so that in this City it is as easy to find a *Steeple* without a Bell hanging in it as a *Vestry* without such a memorial."

A list from the 1400's which does not touch one gift in ten thousands suggests how steadily citizens remembered their towns, to do them good. In London, William Elsing, mercer, founded a hospital for the "sustentation of an hundred poor blind men, and became himself the first prior of that hospital." At Stratford, Hugh Clopton, "during his life a bachelor, mayor 1492," rebuilt the nave of the Guild Chapel and built a fourteen-arch stone bridge over the Avon, still steadily used. Sir Robert Knoles, "citizen, founded a college with a hospital; he also built the great stone bridge at Rochester, over the river of Medway"; and Robert Large, a mercer (to whom Caxton was apprenticed at seventeen), "mayor 1440, gave ... to London bridge one hundred marks, [and] towards the vaulting over the water-course of Walbrooke [a brook through central London to the Thames] two hundred marks." William Eastfield in 1438 left money to make "a fair conduit ... to convey sweet water from Tyborne" into the City, and a fountain near the new Guildhall. (Tyburn brook ran into the Thames below Chelsea.) And John Wells, grocer, mayor in 1433, "caused fresh water to be conveyed from Tyborne [into the City] ... for service of the city." "Simon Eyre, draper, mayor 1446 ... built ... a common garner of corn for the use of this city." Godfrey Bollein, Queen Anne's great-grandfather, in 1457 "by his testament, gave liberally to prisons, hospitals, and lazar houses, besides a thousand pounds to poor householders in London"; a sheriff, Richard Rawson, 1477, left legacies for hospitals, highways, water-conduits, and three hundred forty pounds "to poor maids' marriages."

The record of honor runs on. Richard Whittington, "mercer, three times mayor"—("Turn again, Whittington, Thrice mayor of London," Bow Bells had told him)—in 1421 gave four hundred pounds toward the library of the Grey Friars, founded an almshouse for thirteen poor men, and endowed "divinity lectures to be read there for ever." He "repaired St. Bartholomew's hospital in Smithfield," outside the north wall, "bare half the charges of . . . the library" in the Guildhall then being built (1411-1439), and "built the west gate of London, of old times called Newgate." A goldsmith, Edward Shaw, "newly built of his goods" Cripplegate, the gate to the north, and Thomas Falconar, mercer and mayor in 1414, made the postern called Moorgate, to the North, the last London gate. He also "caused the ditches of the city [the wide moats just outside the walls] to be cleaned, and did many other things for good of the same city." So the list goes on, its repetitions dulling, but emphasizing, what at first were its surprises.

These known names stand for innumerable others: for ordinary men who left no memory but who lived with decency and added to the good fortune of their time; and for the citizens whose care and affection toward the places they were born or had lived make a continuing record in the century.

In the will or the statutes which established his gift a donor often showed a simplicity of faith touching and direct. One donor provided ten teachers for his new college because in his life he had broken all God's Ten Commandments. Another, founding a school, set the number of boys in it at one hundred fifty-three because it was said there were one hundred fifty-three fishes in the Miraculous Draught which Simon Peter drew up in his net out of Gennesaret. A bridge, one donor enjoined, was to be built in three arches as honor to the Trinity. For all things—the martyrs, whales that move in the water, and even the numbers of arithmetic—are means to praise Him and magnify Him forever.

* * * * *

Most material things made in the 1400's are gone. Many have lasted, much or little changed: for instance King's College Chapel at Cambridge, the Chapel of Henry VII in the Abbey, St. George's at Windsor, and other church buildings; some lovely, formal table-silver, illuminations in manuscripts, a good number of books and records and accounts; bridges and walls and rooms and castles and manor houses, and much else. The list seems long; yet what is left now is a small part out of the fifteenth century. Objects of that time are rare nowadays; they did not re-create, as leaves come back on the trees. They were; and a few of them are; but they are not to-be. At best only a copy gets made, and that not often.

What has lasted on—"roots and ever green"—seems to have been the thoughts, perceptions, and feelings which made persons write and build and give as they did. In whatever ways the century expressed itself, back of each expression were the special, compelling qualities of someone—his ideas and ability and will and feeling. These are back of the cathedrals, and Bosworth Field, and the *Morte d'Arthur*. An idea is alive. It can adjust as time goes on. It can vary, enlarge, bear surprising fruit, stay new or fade—adapting, growing, lessening, but not violating its own way. An object, being complete, does not change. It keeps its fixed and final form. At best it will only stay serene as it was made. It does not have eternity. So, looked at through time, Archbishop Rotherham's expressed gratitude for one teacher he had as a green boy; and Caxton's concern that his town have a "well-stuffed lybrayre" are strange only in the spelling.

All this, I suppose, is saying that the spirit is the life of the body, a divine vitality; that only life creates a new life; and that the new always has its own new form, because the power of the spirit is not fulfilled in one expression, in any one embodiment. For the new comes in its course and is right and needed; and it repeats itself, creating another form; and this succession and variety which the spirit creates does not have an end that is seen.

The men and women brought gifts to the towns. Money and buildings were good gifts: they raised the towns; they ornamented a town and expressed it, and gave it strength. So—very much in a final estimate—did the gifts of thought and care and affection—the qualities and purposes that went into the gifts. Those counted; as what counted about the conduits which were given London was the water flowing in them.

London Impressions

Someone imagining London five hundred years ago may see—is likely to see—an outline of climbing fabulous towers which are held in, below, by dark walls and a bright sweep of river, and backed against solidly-blue sky highlighted by lines of gold; a city impossible for human uses; the illumination in a medieval manuscript.

So someone might assume that London was quite different from the rest of England; was beyond the stories told of London successes—beyond even the fairy tale of Whittington, Bow Bells, and the cat. Logic, from a premise of fact, could get the same conclusion. Its size and wealth and first place in business and government, its steady drawing people to it—in fact, its eminence in everything going on in England—would make London incomparable.

* * * * *

So it might seem. Yet the idea is curiously wrong. London was strongly and purely English. If it drew into itself, it gave back; if London was shut in by walls, it kept a keen sense of the country; and if the king and nobles and bishops and the chancellor lived part of their time in London (really, most of them lived in Westminster or Southwark or in the open suburbs beyond the gates), there is plenty of proof they remembered their earlier towns and loved them, and when they could went back to live where they were born.

Indeed, in its aims and acts and customs and history, in its affections and the strength of its opinions, and in its value on business, London was pretty much like other towns. Differences were rather in size than in kind. London had more *amount* of opinion, more *bulk* of trade, with the uniqueness which greater size does bring. London was first, but first among equals. It was never a stranger. It was itself but typical. And a foreigner coming ashore in the Port of London, by the Bridge, knew at first sight (or first smell or sound or tone of voice or first opinion) that he had landed in an English town.

* * * * *

London and the country got on well together. Essentially, they were not opposed in spirit or ways of living. Except perhaps at its center, in the crowded wards close along the river, London had "a semi-rural air." Yet even in the busiest part of London (the Vintners' Ward, a third of a mile west of London Bridge on Thames Street next the river) Chaucer's father—one out of many—built a house flush on the street but having a garden with Walbrook flowing along one side of it. In the century, a coroner's roll shows that a man fell from "a pear tree in a garden" of Vintners' Ward and was killed. Just outside the wall "the merchants," wrote Stowe, "set their shops and houses among gardens and orchards; adjoining to the houses on all sides lie the gardens of these citizens . . . well furnished with trees, spacious and beautiful." London never destroyed the country for the English, as Paris did for the French.

Through London—the City within walls and ditches—flowed streams and brooks and two rivers: Walbrook, arched over in the late 1400's, which cut central London into east and west; and the Fleet, then a navigable river, but now flowing as Baedeker puts it, "in the form of a sewer" to the Thames. Less than a mile from the great wharfs, where five-storey and six-storey warehouses crowded the edge of the river, was open country. Chaucer while he lived in Aldgate on the City wall (from 1374 to 1386) was literally a step from the fields. And two hundred years after Chaucer, Pepys still found open fields—Moorfields—just outside Moorgate. Beyond the wall, east and north and west, the suburbs merged easily into meadows and woods.

Just outside the City wall, even in 1550, Hog Lane, north, beyond Aldergate "had on both sides fair hedge rows of Elm trees, with bridges and easy stiles to pass over into pleasant fields, very commodious for citizens to walk, shoot, and otherwise recreate and refresh their dull spirits in the sweet and wholesome air."

Medieval London lay along the Thames, in shape like a half-disc—its line of diameter the river, its edge the City wall. It was a drawn English bow, with the river the bowstring and the wall the bent bow. It was a half-moon crescent, about one mile and a third from the Tower at the eastern tip to Westminster, and just three-fifths of a mile from the river to the most northern gate, Moorgate. The crowded space between the river and the enclosing wall was a spiderweb of crisscross streets and lanes and four-foot alleys. Brooks and the two streams cut through the City, flowing north to south into the Thames.

* * * * *

By 1450 there were in London probably between fifty thousand and sixty thousand people. Facts about the size of London then are insecure; they leave much margin. (In 1600, with more certainty, London and its suburbs is given two hundred fifty thousand people; in 1666, the year of the Great Fire, there were around three hundred fifty thousand.) The population of England about 1480 seems to have been nearly two and a half million people.

Yet it is clear that London was the central sun for England: five times as large as the second city, York, and larger by ten thousand than the next four—York, Norwich, Chester, Bristol—taken together. It was a great city of Europe; perhaps the third or fourth city of Christendom, close after Paris, Florence, and Bruges and Ghent in Flanders.

It was the richest city in Europe; the English, at any rate, were sure that "richer resteth under no Christian King." The wealth of its citizens amazed foreigners. In 1466 an Italian (Dominic Mancini) lists, among much else, that London traded in wines, minerals, ship supplies (timber, flax, tar, ropes), grain, fish, coal, all manner of woven goods, "gold and silver cups . . . silk, carpets, tapestry, and much other exotic merchandise." London, said another traveller about 1490, had two hundred master goldsmiths. Another, an Italian, wrote that in one street—probably Cheapside—"I have found fifty-two goldsmiths' shops so rich and full of silver vessels, great and small, that in all the shops of Milan, Rome, Venice, and Florence put together, I do not think there would be found so many. . . . There is nowhere lack of anything." Even the apprentices seemed more boisterous, more full-blooded and opinionated, more alert at work. This was the opulent London; and it was not merely a surface.

London-born

Except Colet and Whittington, most Londoners we know best from the 1400's were not born in London. Caxton was out of the Weald of Kent ("I . . . was born & lerned myne Englissh in kente in the weeld"). Richard Pace seems to have come from Winchester: there, he says, he was "a boy among boys"—*puerum inter pueros.* Malory was born in Warwickshire; Rolle of Hampole and Rotherham in Yorkshire; Richard III at Fotheringay Castle in Northamptonshire; and Suffolk "at his father's manor house of Cotton in Suffolk." No English king of the century and no great noble was a Londoner by birth and breeding, and few in the Church or in government were. On the list of benefactors to London few native Londoners are named. One is hard-set to find among the best-known London men of the 1400's as many as a half-dozen who were London-born.

The River

London was centered, fed, made beautiful and rich, and in many ways controlled by the great river, which flowing out of the country brought with it the certainty and tone of its origin; and carried into the Channel and the Atlantic and the North Sea and the Mediterranean (to Flanders, and Russia and Africa and Constantinople and, once at least, to the unnamed new continent) the commerce and the adventurers of fifteenth-century England.

For one thing, the river—"this moste pleasant fludde"—had the greatest practical use. It had founded the city and had built it into the London which the English were sure (and foreigners half-allowed) was "the *second* City in Christendome for *greatness,* and the *first* for *good Government.* There is no civilized part of the World but . . . hath heard thereof, though many . . . conceive *London* to be the Country, and *England* but the City therein. . . . It oweth its greatness, under God's divine providence, to the well-conditioned River of Thames, which doth not (as some Tyrant Rivers in Europe) abuse its strength in a destructive way, but implyeth its *greatness in goodness,* to be beneficial for commerce, by the reciprocation [the ebb and flow] of the Tide therein."

And the river was (at another extreme of human interest) a friend to poets and other adventurers. William Dumbar the poet, in the 1400's, wrote of the freshness, grace, loveliness the Thames brought to London. "Fresh is thy ryver . . . pleasaunt and preclare [very clear], Under thy lusty wallys [it] runneth down, Where many a swan doth swymme with wyngis fair."

Country winds and smells, and country birds and flowers and trees came into the city, into the streets and squares and gardens. Townspeople knew this. Even into the crowded parts along the river, the "fields breathe sweet . . . In every street these tunes our ears do greet—*Cuckoo, jug-jug, pu-we, to-witta-woo!*" Exaggerated no doubt, yet a truth — though enlarged — of fifteenth-century London.

The Thames, flowing out to the ocean, joined Londoners—a few at least—to places beyond Italy and the Capes of Spain; and to adventure, imagination, action, and wealth. (It had brought those to others.) So the river was to most in the town their provider; and their intimate, good, kindly friend—really an interesting news-bringer and gossip. And to a few—the imaginers—it was a province of the unknown, a half-assurance to them of the impossible, a way into wonders.

3

THREE CURRENTS

In fifteenth-century England strong currents of progress ran. Learning was moving from scholasticism into humanism—into the brightness of the Renaissance. A middle class was growing up between nobles and peasants. And national unity was sweeping over England, deepening as the century went on; the English, though they did not see it, were getting to be of one blood.

I. Scholasticism and Humanism

Scholasticism accepted, quite literally and completely, the authority of the book; of the ancient book—the Bible, Aristotle, the Church Fathers, Latin classics; "olde fieldes" out of which, Chaucer had written, comes all the new corn. From those books it took mainly rules and facts and language. Humanism liked old books and it liked its own time; it wanted to bring together the old books and the present world. It was sure the old books were alive. The humanist was hoping to unite today and the time gone by; to bring freshly into his own city Aristotle and the Bible; to, for one thing, find and follow Virgil and poetry. If the humanist did not deeply question the past, he did look back into it and realize and enjoy it, and he looked at his own people and their affairs. He held the classics were part of the past and of the present, joining the life and learning and language and art of the two.

The center of scholastic study was *grammar* and *theology*. Grammar meant knowing the Latin language. Latin was the aim and end of the schools. By it all knowledge was gained and taught, and passed from scholar to scholar, and from one nation to another. Oxford, Paris, Rome, Constantinople through it might understand each other. The Humanists, too, held that *grammar* was the center of study, the mother and cherisher of learning, its beginning and its strength—*initium et fundamentum*. That is, a scholar must speak and read and write Latin fluently and with discrimination. But the humanist turned his Latin to his purpose. He often used *literature* in place of *grammar,* holding the words to lead toward the same end (and later, he joined *manners*—conduct—with the two). A schoolman held such use a gross error, for surely *grammar* was definitions, rules and form, the giving of examples, the picking out of phrases that illustrated style and prosody. *Grammar* was not a means to feel or touch or record shapes and identities in a world passing today or in one that had passed at Rome, in Caesar's time. It was not to record the flow of life.

Early Latin textbooks show this spirit. They are in structure and substance "a maddening mixture," a rabble of rules set down in doggeral Latin verse. The first differing English-Latin grammar came about 1457, and close to 1500 William Lyly, a young Oxford humanist and a teacher at St. Paul's, London, made a Latin grammar of the same new sort (Erasmus and Colet had a hand in the book), which "ruled the schools of England to the middle of the nineteenth century."

Scholastic *theology* held its interest on the heaven and hell to come after this life's pilgrimage. Not life, not how to live, but how to be ready for death was the great cause and substance of its study. The humanist, too, thought of the eternal life he must enter, but more often he looked at the level, human, open world.

And, as humanists saw it, your schoolman came near to worshipping the forms of expression—the wording of a classic, and the methods of logic. The truth and the implications of a statement in the Bible or in Plato or even in a bestiary were to stand not questioned. "It is written there" ended questioning and mystery. It was the final, lasting, settling answer. Schoolmen gave much attention to forms of statement; to, for one thing, dialectics. Dialectics came for them to mean an intricate and minute analysis— microscopic logic. Such analysis the humanist did not care for. He used and valued analysis for its result; for its answer to *what* and *why*. He was sure that acrobatics of logic got lost in showmanship; and that the method, the "administration," surely shut out the coming of truth. The humanist insisted logic should not be put on display. He wanted "more matter with less art."

Humanism was a quality of taste and mind and a custom of action; hardly a moral quality. Sir Thomas More and humanists like him did see by a moral light within them, but some others coolly disregarded morality or had primitive ignorance of good and evil. A king's general is said to have suffered more at the sight of a torn manuscript than of a burning town; and the brother of Henry V, the Good Duke Humphrey of Gloucester (rather a scoundrel, all told), built his library of six hundred volumes ("the finest in Europe, with its gorgeously illuminated manuscripts bound in gem-encrusted covers") from the looting of French towns.

In England there were many with a pure flame. There were Colet, the Lady Margaret Beaufort (in 1485 the mother of the King), Erasmus, Richard Pace, Caxton, Mallory, Rolle of Hampole a little earlier; and—possibly less, from being much occupied with affairs of government—Thomas Rotherham, Lord Rivers (a great scholar and churchman and author and gentleman), the poor King Henry VI (with Eton and King's College to his credit), and even Wolsey, who, to his credit, had Hampton Court—which is humanistic, if a place can be. In the century there were many—perfect and imperfect in wide gradation—to witness for this faith.

Erasmus, "the most cultured and learned of his time," asked: "What hath nature ever fashioned softer, or sweeter, or pleasanter than the disposition of Sir Thomas More?" Erasmus was twelve years older than More. His *In Praise of Folly*, which More put from Latin into English, is a graceful, gay, wise, and polished book, quite the spirit of humanism. Largely, the writing in this century is that sort. It is romantic, serene, hopeful, secure, in its purpose, without the violence of later revolt. Revolt was more spoken and acted than written. Books of the time were likely to touch the wonders of lands and oceans and sky just being discovered, and the wonder of the classics—especially the Greek—then newly realized.

This English humanism had in it an impulse to patriotism. Humanists loved old writing, but they wrote new books. They found in the classics the spirit and impulse of truth. Homer and Virgil looked squarely at what was to be seen around them; and by their imagination they looked at what was not to be seen. A humanist wanted to write that way. He hoped to tell what was present to his eyes and to his mind—his seen and unseen—in a book which he would not have been ashamed to have Homer or Virgil read; at least, not ashamed of its purpose. Humanists wanted to find and make alive something true, as the ancients had; but their own voices were to be heard—no echo. They wrote not in defiance of the old but in agreement with the present; of which—by body and spirit and speech—each of them felt he was a part.

II.   The Rise of the Middle Class

Yeoman

The word *yeoman,* from 1300 to 1600, had a dozen separate meanings, and one general meaning which changed in the two centuries, though always *yeoman* stayed very English. The definition had to be wide because the word covered a class with vitality enough for many differences, and the energy for change. *Yeoman,* about 1400, meant *servant;* and there agreement broke. A yeoman was a menial servant on an estate (Chaucer's yeoman was a first-rate woodsman, "a forester"); at Court or in a noble household, he was the young aspirant only a step below the squire—a servant but serving his lord.

By the later 1400's *yeoman* (except for those in special service at Court—Yeoman of the Guard, of the Wardrobe, of the Body) was coming pretty generally to mean a small freeholder or a renter of land who had money enough; whom the land did not own. He was, too, a small tradesman, a man in a profession, a steward or agent or factor, the owner of a ship, or anyone else who worked for himself or with much freedom. Most often in the century he was thought of (and idealized) as the English foot soldier, such as fought at Agincourt or had been a bowman at Crecy. A yeoman fighting came to be England fighting. (The English hated mercenary soldiers. They had contempt for the French as long as the best French troops were hired archers from Genoa or Scotland.) A writer of the century puts it: *If the yeoman of England were not in time of war, we should be in shrewd case. For in them stands the chief defense of England.*

In spite of their wide range, the word and the class stood clearly for qualities: for independence perhaps first, and reliability, and steady unspectacular good sense, and enough boldness for action. The circle of meaning had widened from men of small and usual successes to include a fairly rich merchant and an officer of the Church and of government. However far the term reached out, it meant character, ability, and some success. By 1450 it named a class which was hard to define but had clear meaning for the times.

Four hundred years after 1450 a yeoman still was held admirably and typically English in body and spirit. He had grown older and was back from war, but he was a good fellow and a fighter. In *Lavengro,* 1859, George Borrow, praising someone he liked (a retired prize fighter, who kept an inn near London), called him "the yeoman . . . sharp as winter, kind as spring . . . honest John Bull . . . 'We shan't find such another . . . Old England his mother.'"

Four hundred years before *Lavengro* and a hundred years after, the word meant much the same.

The Middle Class As a Whole

Yeoman were a part of the middle class, a lesser rank in its wide, undefined range. In the middle class were great city merchants; wealthy franklins in the country; students, clerks, and men of the professions; guildsmen and craftsmen and stewards. Indeed, by 1500 it covered most of those above poverty but not drawing incomes from estates, or from high offices in the Church or high positions in government or at Court. It emerged in England, where feudalism was not the form of society, and where chances—small and large—lay open in business, the Church, professions, government, war, and even at Court. In the 1400's it was the class increasingly "thrust between lord and peasant and coming to its own," often with struggle and pain.

First and last, the successes of middle class men—to take them, unfairly, as a whole—did not require genius or court favor or wealth or noble birth. Their success took intelligence, tenacity, work, honesty, some gifts but much obstinacy, mother wit, self-direction and self-control, and a good body—solid if not shining qualities; yeomen qualities largely, it seems.

The qualities brought defects—arrogance certainly, narrow tastes and sympathies, hard morality, a lack of delight and depth and peace. Still, in the long run, they were very good to have even when diluted. They were, in a term of the wool trade, "ingrain." They would "endure wind and weather." Probably no one of the middle class had them all; yet all of them fused in the ideal middle-class Englishman.

Even a fair share of them seems to have got men ahead. They were the qualities of the good, level, middle-class citizens; for generations in medieval England the steady, stubborn, capable, fairly educated, fairly intelligent followers of the middle way—of the golden mean, perhaps.

And when a man of the middle class came to a high position, as many of them did, he seems to have kept his qualities. Usually he carried his success evenly and well; not always, as Wolsey—"a butcher's son"—was to show (but not all those in any class ever have kept altitude), and even he seems to have been ready to acknowledge "from whence he had his Rise." A bishop, born "a poor boy," in a sermon before the King told that when he was a child his mother milked thirty cows each morning. Archbishop Rother-

41

ham of York founded the College of Jesus at Rotherham, the town where he had been born, "in gratitude," he wrote, that, though ignorant and "rude," through "God's will I have arrived at the estate in which I now have come." Edmund Bonner, Bishop of London (John Aubrey wrote), "at first a skullion boy in the kitchin [at Oxford, in the 1400's], when he came to his greatness, in ac- knowledgment . . . gave to the kitchin there a great brase-pott, called Bonners-pott . . . Mr. Steevens has shewed the Pott to me. It was the biggest, perhaps, in Oxford."

III. Nationalism

England in the 1400's was growing to be a nation. Class and work and wealth and education and distance did divide. Clearly, an earl, a poor scholar, a bishop, a cobbler, a goldsmith, a forester, a wandering juggler was just that; and York was a long way from London. Yet, just as clearly—though they did not often see it— they were close to one another, helping and hurting one another, and all having common interests and traits and beliefs and one inherited English history. It was a kind of democracy, if not social equality.

They were, too, recognizing, at least now and then and in the large, that other persons were individuals. They saw each other. They did not always like what they saw, or act justly. Yet national- ity increased in the century, and the right to individuality (in some ways its opposite) was more allowed. The War of the Roses was fought by feuding princes, not by the divided nation. The English in their relations to each other and to the central state were better off than any other people in Europe.

Slowly—very slowly at best—this enlargement into unity went on. After 1485, that is after the death of Richard at Bosworth Field, even nobles whose quarreling had made the War were recognizing they were part of a nation. Not to see this intimacy and interplay among classes and persons (and still see their differences and divisions) is to miss what was happening in English life; what was moving, then, on the face of the waters.

This union and separateness—lessening and increasing, realized and unseen—had been going on in England long before the fif- teenth century, and went on centuries after. In the 1300's, Chau- cer's pilgrims showed their unlikeness and their likeness. It is easily clear that the Miller, the Somonour, the Monk, the Wife of Bath are primary and real, are strikingly defined; and that physic- ally and in mind and manners and morals (though some kept the law and some broke it), all of them, good and bad and high and low, belonged in England. They could never have come from anywhere else: not from France or Italy or the Imagined Mountains. Mallory's knights are English.

This personal independence (the certainty of oneself and reliance on oneself) and this common Englishness cut across the classes. The century was likely to accept, as natural to mankind, that a person might be strikingly and boldly himself. A nobleman might or might not know how to read and write and even the king might be a scholar or an ignoramus; the royal chancellor might be the son of an earl or of no blood. "The Commons" as a term gathered into itself without incongruity to anyone, a merchant who lent the king nine hundred thousand pounds, the greenest apprentice, and the freeholder with small land and a cart. The term seems to have stopped only with the leper and the beggar on the road. A freeman had a right to be himself.

And in the century they were—or were moving to be—all English. They held together, give and take; not perfectly or peacefully, and with much frank speech and heavy silence of opposition, and with some bloody fighting; but on the whole they did hold together.

Such belief in himself and in England was strong through later English history. Elizabeth, a hundred years after Mallory and two hundred after Chaucer, told her Parliament that—their annointed queen—she yet thanked God that if she "were sent out of the realm in her petticoat" she could make her way. She was sure of her "qualities"; of her rights as a person and their queen. She stood as "God had been pleased to make her." She was equally sure that among God's gifts to her she valued most of all that she was purely English. Forty-two years later, toward the end, when she was sixty-eight, she said much the same again: "This I count the glory of my crown—that I have reigned with your love." This steady belief, the seventeenth century got by inheritance; to which the 1400's added.

Other nations thought the English were united. They thought them all self-satisfied, bragging, quarrelsome even among themselves. The Venetian envoy to Henry VIII wrote back to Venice, "the English are great lovers of themselves and of anything belonging to them; they think there are no other men than themselves and no other world but England." They were pleased with their own, sure of their clothes and their opinions, hard to get along with, "as if England were the whole world." No other land

43

could hold a candle to theirs. The traits were rasping and unlovely, but they helped build the nation. And so, they helped build up the parts of the English nation—government, trade, the army and navy, ways of life in the town and the country, music, education, the universities, and much else that made the likeness of England.

England never had been a feudal state, or a shifting association of princes or cities or provinces, or had its boundaries fixed by a royal marriage. It had inherent stability. On the island the boundaries of England had not changed in four hundred years.

People in the century were seldom conscious of their union. It was around them, but unfocused. It was their climate. Though they did not talk of it or see it, it gave life to their political and social worlds. It had grown by adjustments through centuries. It was a way of living, which had been worked out over a long time, by instinct and practical trial. If it did not have the cool, beautiful certainty of mathematics, it did have durability. Generally it worked; and when it did not work it could be changed, for it was not beyond question and attack, and change. It had the energy and endurance of a tough natural growth. At its best there was in it something of the pliancy, the power to adapt, which will be in a family where there is respect and tolerance and good purpose, and, at its best, love. In spite of stupidity and violence and the heavy weight of custom, there was growing in England, with life-giving power, both the reliance of one man on another and the granting to him of space to be himself.

England was becoming a nation, an imperfect union but genuine and strong. It is impossible to isolate the causes of this into facts and dates. The unity came out of the instincts and ideals of the English, and their ways of living for six hundred years. It was a growth of English qualities; a climate they lived in because they breathed best in it; and being intangible and air, it is hard to diagram. Their instinct for nationality was like a force of nature which completes itself in fertility. It was the sap which engendered the flower, the spirit fulfilling itself.

To follow, fact by fact, the flow of English history to 1500, and to believe this is finding the causes and current of English nationalism is twice a fool's journey. Nationalism is too fluid and human for success in such pursuit. The start of an effect—the far-off first energy—is hidden, or known by faith; and the chain of linked, explanatory events from first to last is not easy to show. In a simple, physical process it seems fair to say that *this* came after *that;* and that the first was needed for the second. A simple progression may be quite clear up to the end, but the end, the discovery, is likely to open into an unknown ocean. Many times a new question is there; to be acknowledged, and accepted with grace as a mystery. "To know, can only wonder breede," wrote Sidney Godolphin, a Lord Commissioner of the Treasury for Charles II.

Yet it is clear enough that in the 1400's some definite and lasting influences still were increasing the stability of the nation, as they had for centuries: the geography of England, for instance, and the character of the king. And, too, an act done on one day and at one place, a decision, something said or written affected the whole body of England. It brought a force into focus, and so, brought change. The printing of the first English book with the date in it did that, November 18, 1477. So did Henry VII's winning at Bosworth, August 22, 1485.

Through the uneasy century (and the 1400's were not passive) nationalism grew. Questions were being asked by persons and by the conditions in England. One question was: *Who make up the nation?* And, in a hesitant, blurred, inexpert way the time was beginning to think over—but only a little—the place of the king's sacred authority, and the place of shires and towns and citizens; and what should be the substance of the laws, and how laws were to be made, and how they were to be administered. Some kept writing about their One Church, and about the part the clergy were having in government and even in business. A few wondered whether force did settle a question. The English were growing inquisitive about matters which made up the fabric of England.

At times and places that can be fixed some of the questions got some sort of answer: a confused, trial one, often wrong, but an answer. Some answers—but with new questions implied—were the Peasants' Revolt, the deposition of Henry VI, the triumph of Joan of Arc. These events can be "spotted" exactly; can be dated as clearly as D-Day can. Indeed, some of them have a clear, dramatic course of *start, progress, curtain.*

These questions and these events help to show what sort of people the English were in the 1400's. They show qualities and powers and purposes, and how people carried out their purposes. They show people moving ahead in their lives by their decisions and actions. Yet not one of their actions is a complete, clear-cut, single, self-bounded cause. Each act or thought is both a beginning and an end; a part; a point in the unbroken line of fifteenth-century history.

I think a practical man and a mystic might agree, though each would use his own words, that a cause may become an end, which in its turn may become a cause again.

Probably, to most English people in the 1400's a national event —when at last they heard of it—seemed far away; as indeed it was for them. It is uncommon for anyone to realize the main currents of the time which is flowing past him. It is rare—possible, but very rare—for him to see the force and significance of an incident which has just happened. His own life—so close to him—is a full occupation. The immediate beat and lift of personal happiness; the tension of going ahead; or—an opposite—the torpor of day by day repetition, engulfs him. His training and ideals and logic may, too, add a coefficient to what he sees going on, change its value, and so, give a wrong answer. And time gets in the way of judgment. What is held close to the eyes may seem unreally large or be a bright blur of color. Or a judgment made long after an event may make an opposite distortion; the reality may have shrunk in size; grown dim; hardened to a memory.

History

Their history—what they had been in time long ago and in time just past—bound the English together. The course of the Hundred Years War in France shows one proof of this. The War began with a rush of victories in the 1340's and ended in steady loss of French territory and clear defeat. By 1451 only Calais was left.

If the long war did nothing else, it brought the English to know one another, and to trust one another's honesty and energy and strength, because the War had proved them. At first, in the 1340's, the glory of immediate success (Crecy was won in 1346) was dazzling. It drew them together in pride, assurance, and wealth—for at first the fighting did enrich and excite the kingdom. Agincourt, in 1456, renewed their certainty of themselves. And at the end, forty years later, they were—unknowingly and bitterly and in spite of their humiliation and helplessness and anger, and the political confusion at home—even more a nation.

Ten thousand other happenings in their history helped them see that they were, truly, alike in their spirit and purposes and needs, and—largely—in their ways of deciding and acting.

Geography

Four main facts in the geography of England were: the ocean, which bounded nine-tenths of England; the Gulf Stream, which brought moisture and warmth; the absence of barriers to cut the land apart; and the harbors, and the streams, and the large rivers —the Severn, the Mersey, the Tyne, the Humber, and the Thames. All affected national unity (some very much, some less strongly), but the ocean had most force.

Fifteenth-century Englishmen were conscious of the sea. It was close by; constant; literally nowhere more than seventy miles away. To most of them the winds and smells and sounds of the ocean were familiar all their lives. They did not write much about the ocean. Caxton, Mallory, even Mandeville, were not by nature seamen.

From first to last, and in spite of seeing the contrary, they were confident that the sea was their protection, an enclosing safety, a moat, a wall; and that it would be an active help when the need came. They had learned its power and wilfulness, and their condition: "Who hath gathered the wind in his fist? Who can bind the waters?" The Church had prayers for those in peril at sea. Still, they did not doubt that the ocean would rise in a great danger and their enemy be scattered. "Like as the smoke vanisheth, so shalt thou drive them away!"

For the ocean was a friend. It took their ships and fishing vessels out and usually brought them back, and it carried their navy. It gave them food. It was an open road to France and Flanders, and to Italy and Spain farther off, and to Constantinople and Russia and the world's end. They liked to watch the ocean. They liked the sight of the "triumphant billows." It was a silver sea, in which fortunately their land was set.

Town and Country

In spite of differences, town and country were close in ways of living and in interests. Of the—possibly—2,500,000 people in England, nine-tenths lived on the land and the rest kept close association with it. They looked at a horizon more than at walls. Besides the great town of London, only York in the North, Bristol with western and ocean commerce, and Norwich, the center of wool trade to the Continent, came near ten thousand people. Hardly a dozen towns had four thousand.

But the unity of town and country was not won on a majority. It was a union of love. The English—nobles to plowmen and apprentices—were at home and happy in the country. Fields came, for townsmen, close up to the walls; and townsmen who had the money liked the house with a garden "banking on the river." Ad-

47

venturing young men who came to town to make their fortunes often found, after the first excitement of novelty and perhaps of success, that however dazzling it all was, they remembered the open spaces of field and sky outside the town. And old, wealthy, well-established merchants were likely to go back from their success to the old places; as William Grevel did to Oxfordshire; and Thomas Rotherham, the King's Chancellor and Archbishop, to Yorkshire; and Hugh Clopton, London mercer, to Stratford; and, for that matter, as later Shakespeare did. When they stayed in London, they might have a house and garden close to a stream. In the 1400's brooks still were flowing through the town. Chaucer was born in mid-London, but his father's house was backed by a garden with Walbrook for its east boundary.

No one, of course, went about always thinking country thoughts and dreaming the idyllic. Yet it is impossible to understand the century without realizing that English people then, in temper and fact, lived close to open fields and forests and streams and other country sights and influences, and that, gentle or simple, they liked the country ways—its beasts and sports and work, and country weather, and country food and talk and songs. Fortunately, the English towns did have easy access to the country around them. Fortunately, too, English towns never were centered in themselves and enemies to one another, as German, Spanish, and Italian towns were apt to be.

A formal symbol of unity—suggestion, not proof—may be the arms of the four large towns. Each bears a national emblem, and a charge which shows the special strength of the town. Norwich has on a red shield "a castle triple-towered argent, in base a lion of England." The other three display the Red Cross of St. George (for England) and a local mark: London, St. Peter's sword in red; York, three lions in gold; Bristol, a silver-domed castle by water, and on the water a three-masted golden ship with a silver sail.

Travel

In the 1400's traveling was easier. Roads and bridges and fords and the inns were better cared for, and the King's Peace was better kept on the highway though still not secure. The strong, stone-made Roman roads, built twelve hundred years before, still were very good roads. They centered at London, and ran west, and northwest to the Atlantic, and straight north to the Border: Watling Street and Foss Way out into the west, and Ermine Way north to York and beyond. The Roman roads had strange names; "fantastic names"; so corrupted by time and use that the origin of none of them is certain.

The later roads, though old in the 1400's—the pilgrims' way to Canterbury or to St. Mary of Walsingham, and to the hundred lesser shrines—were well kept. Still newer roads had been made, which in dry weather were firm enough for carts, and even in wet times gave footing for pack horses that carried much of the English goods. In this century the highways seemed to have been better looked after than in Elizabeth's time, two hundred years later.

Most of the large towns made steady use of waterways—their navigable rivers and the ocean. York had the Ouse and the North Sea; Norwich, its river and the Sea; Bristol, the Severn, all the Atlantic if it wanted, and the Channel south around Land's End, and the Bay of Biscay far south. The Thames was London's way out into the world.

By land or water, travel was quicker than it ever had been, though in 1483, when Edward IV died, a messenger posthaste from London to the King's brother needed six days to ride a hundred ninety miles. In the earlier 1500's it took nine days to sail from Southampton across and down the Channel to Spain; with storms it took six weeks or all the summer. Horseback—the usual way—with a good road thirty-five miles a day was steady, determined riding. In the *Paston Letters* that seems the average of many journeys. Thirty miles was acceptable. Chaucer's Canterbury pilgrims, one supposes, took two or three days each way (London to Canterbury was sixty-three miles), but they went at a holiday pace, three miles or so an hour, with much talk and stopping. Chaucer tells of their starting from the Tabard Inn: *And forth we riden, a litel moore than pass*—a little more than a walk. With fortune one might ride from Norwich to London, one hundred twenty-five miles, in about four days.

It was only the main roads that were fairly cared for—marked, surfaced (in a way), bridged, and guarded. Lesser roads—roads less near London and the great shrines, and less-used for trade; that is, most roads—were likely to be thin tracks on high ground (safer from flooding), not much marked or looked after or fixed to one course. They might be bogged down by rain, gullied, rutted to impassibility, ground into dust inches deep, grown back into the moor or to the field, or pre-empted—often by a great landowner. Sometimes, travelers had to take a local guide to find them the course of the road—so vague, so easily lost.

Travel was safer. Yet a private journey or a trading trip was a risk and a discomfort, and slow; and if it was to a faraway place and long and unusual, it was a formidable risk—a recognized and insurable risk of at least five to one against return. Some journeys, surprisingly long in time and miles were undertaken. Such long travel was sure to be full of astonishments and great marvels.

Out of strange journeys, some even in England, grew strange tales told at home ("travellers' tales" Shakespeare calls them): of Prester John's empire, where the phoenix was and the Arabian Tree; of "barking Scylla ... and such like great and incredible monster" off Sicily; of "the great serpents in waste places of Lancashire," which, on their backs, spit poison to the flying larks "to kill them"; of the gay, leaping display of many-colored dolphins in tropic seas; of the *aspic* (carved with authority, in stone, on Amiens Cathedral), a guileful kind of dragon, which could only be caught by singing; of the white, gentle, noble, mystical unicorn; and of an incredible creature like an antelope, the *yale,* which, when it wanted to, could wave its antlers and circle them about—for homage, it was said, to virtue.

Language

"[W]e englysshe men ben borne vnder the domynacyon of the mone, whiche is neuer stedfaste," Caxton wrote in the preface to his *Eneydos.* Their language at least, he thought, followed the moon's changes, "euer wauerynge" but "neuer stedfaste." In 1490 he found that speech was different from what he had spoken when he was a boy, and was not the same from shire to shire. "In so much that in my days, it happened that certain merchants were in a ship in the Thames for to have sailed over the sea to Zelande, and for lack of wind they tarried ... and went on land to refresh them. And one of them named Sheffelde, a mercer, came into a house and asked for meat, and especially he asked after *eggys.* And the good wife answered that she could speak no French. And the merchant was angry, for he also could speak no French, but would have had eggs and she understood him not. And then at last another said that he would have *eyren.* Then the good wife said that she understood him well. Lo, what should a man in these days now write, *egges* or *eyren?*"

The question was real and perplexing. Still, out of time and changing conditions an English language was taking form. Hard divisions of dialect, and separation by class or county were breaking down a little—a very little it seemed to those writing.

Yet a common English was coming into use. There was more cer-

50

tainty that Latin was not the only language for writing, and French not the only speech of a gentleman. All over England people were talking English of a sort, and very much was being written in English—laws and wills and chronicles and government matters, letters and business papers, religious homilies and sermons and *penses* and church records, poetry (songs, tales, ballads), travels, and the *Morte d'Arthur, Mandeville,* and Caxton's books. The extent and variety of the writing is astonishing, but so, too, is the variety of the English used.

The spreading dominance of the East Midland dialect, spoken in London, helped in this gain. It was largely spoken, too, at Oxford and Cambridge, and had the prestige of being spoken at Court. From such use, and from the need of a common language, and from the fresh pleasure it gave, English gained in extent and exactness and authority. More and more people, even those who commonly talked in their local ways, were getting the idea and the sound and the sight of a fairly standard speech.

Latin, in one way an enemy, helped. English valued and used—though transformed—the clearness and exactness and flow of sentences in Latin, and its sense of rhythm and sound. French helped by its wide vocabulary, its easy and exact grammar, its freedom with idioms, and its un-Teutonic way of forming a new word. All these statements need to be adjusted by qualifications and most of them lessened, for close likeness of pronunciation or of phrasing or even of the words spoken in York and Devon and London was hard to find. Yet the English did talk to one another and the one understood what the other said. Their talk was taking on likeness. Most parts of England kept a dialect but were gaining a language.

The best prose of the 1400's, judged by itself as prose, ranks high. Mallory, Wycliffe, More, and Colet witness for the century. Caxton said what he had to say in clear, sharp, easy prose—a pure expression, not contorted in grammar or phrases. His prose lights an idea or a scene into reality, and it characterizes with insight, humor, and sympathy. There is proof for good prose in much plain and usual writing—in letters, sermons, laws, wills, chronicles, and government archives.

The growth of an English language had been going on a long time; indeed, from the Conquest. The merging of Saxon and Norman-French after 1066 is much-told history. Henry III in 1258 issued the first royal proclamation in English: a purely political move with no effect on the language, yet a formal recognition. By 1400 the law courts of Richard II and the Henrys, Chaucer's poetry, and Wycliffe had given English standing and legal authority. Before 1346 Rolle of Hampole said he wrote for those who knew only English. In 1362 the Chief Justice, Sir Henry Green, opened Parliament with a speech in English, and the same Parliament decreed that all pleading and judgment in the law courts should be given in English and enrolled in English. *Men of lawe shold plede in her moder tunge*—in their mother tongue. And in 1484, by a decree of the only Parliament of Richard II, for the first time the English laws were published in English. Schools for boys increased in the 1400's. To enter a grammar school or even an elementary "song-school," a boy must know his English.

Probably, Edward III in the 1300's did not speak or write or read English. Henry IV seems to have used French. Henry V (1413-1422) "wrote letters in good plain English"; though quite different from plain English today. The first part of a letter written by Henry V in 1418 to the Bishop of Durham is this:

> Worschipful fader in God, right trusty and wel beloved...our wel-beloved squier John Hull haath long tyme be in our ambassiat and seruice in the parties of Spaigne, for the whiche, as he haath compleined to us, he is endaungered gretly, and certein goodys of his leyd to wedde...

Slowly in the 1400's more and more people of every class were coming to read and write a fairly common language. A merchant and his clerk, an estate steward, government employees, and many besides scholars and churchmen wrote such English; plus, often, Latin enough for their needs. The Pastons through all the century wrote to one another in clear, ready English.

In the list of citizens who in the 1400's had benefited London was this entry:

> Rober Fabian, alderman, and one of the Sheriffs, 1494, gathered out of divers good authors, as well Latin as French, a large Chronicle of England...which he published *in English*, to his great charges [cost], for the honour of this city, and the common utility of the whole realm.

Printing

In 1477, in Westminster at the sign of the Red Pale, just opposite the Abbey to the west and inside its precincts, Caxton published the first book printed in England. By the end of 1491 he had published ninety. During his life his books were being read all over England and the continent. They brought knowledge to many readers, and helped and pleased the learned (or most of them), and gave chances for the pure joy of reading.

Caxton's books have affected everyone who has lived since they were published. Printing is a primary force, good or bad; as climate is and soil and the use of steam or electricity or the atom. It has given increased force to the purposes of men. It has given a wider range to men's expression.

The books he printed seem to have reached and satisfied people in the 1400's. For one thing printed books were accessible. They came out in many copies, and they were cheap. A book cost one-tenth of what a manuscript cost. And a printed book was exactly like its original. The reproduction was absolute. Each manuscript had been a new copy, a special and fresh hand-transcription, and open to the scrivener's—the professional copyist's—moods of attention, and his ignorance and interest and skill. An inattentive, dumb-witted, wandering copyist might be utter exasperation to a cherisher of his own words. Chaucer in *Unto Adam, His Own Scriveyn,* wished Adam a scabby scalp—"the scalle"—unless

> ...after my making thou wryte trewe.
> So ofte a daye I mot [must] they werk renewe,
> Hit to correcte and eek to rubbe and scrape.
> And al is through they negligence and rape [hurry].

For Adam, it can be said—yet not lessening his sin toward Chaucer—that his pay was twopence a day, the pay of a country carter.

People of the time liked Caxton's books for what was in them: for what they told, and the way they told it; their substance, and tone; the "story," and the "moral" which any writer gets into his book whether he wants to or not. Caxton's books seemed worth reading. They were genuinely popular. People bought them.

He published *The Canterbury Tales* in two editions, the second with illustrations; the *Morte d'Arthur;* two editions of his first book, *Dictes or Sayengis of the Philosophres;* two of *The Golden Legend*—the lives of all the saints; two of *The Game and Playe of the Chesse;* four of *Cato* in different forms (moral maxims in verse, easy to remember); at least a dozen or so books of courtesy and manners and morals for the young; and books about Jason and Aeneas and much else of wide and honest interest, old and new.

Caxton believed earnestly that what he printed would lessen ignorance and so raise and strengthen the qualities of the time; would, he says, "enlighten" England. There was still "much need for people to know"; and so, he would publish good books which should sustain the mind and the conscience of Englishmen; which should increase the nobility of their living. This seems his steady purpose.

In the preface to his *Caton* he wrote that a good book would "remain ever for all people to learn from, and to know from it how every man ought to rule and govern himself . . . as wel for the lyf temporall as for the lyf spyrytual." Such a book, he thought the best book for a little child to learn from in school, "and also [for] peple of euery age . . . yf it be wel understanden."

It is fortunate that Caxton had reasonable wealth and had connection with business and the Church. It is fortunate that Edward IV and the Queen and Earl Rivers had great interest in learning and the arts, and in the new printing, and that when Henry VII came, in 1485, his mother, Margaret Beaufort, a humanist and a very noble lady and of great influence, became Caxton's patron.

It is fortunate—in a material way—that paper had become a common import of England. Until about 1250 vellum (sheepskin) had been used for manuscripts and even for letters. Paper "was one of the conveniences of life for which we are indebted to the Crusades."

Some sheets of the paper on which the Pastons wrote their letters are rough and coarse-fibered; some are admirably smooth in their texture. All of the paper the Pastons used must have been foreign-made. Papermaking did not begin in England until close to 1500.

The Wool Trade

The wool trade, prime and princely occupation of England, brought together landholders, banker-goldsmiths and small traders, weavers (most of them isolated in villages and in hidden, far-off farms), clothworkers of the towns, packmen on the roads, shipmen to carry the wool and cloth, innkeepers, government clerks, factors in Bruges and Calais, nobles, the Church, Parliament: everybody. It kept supremacy until coal and iron changed the center of power. Other trades were nowhere.

The trade touched many people, partly because there were many processes in it, most of them done best by one person. The sheep needed care, good pasture, and skillful shearing. After the shearing came carding the wool, spinning into yarn, weaving, fulling (thickening; giving body to), cloth-shearing, dyeing. Last was the storing and marketing and the distributing in England or the shipping to Flanders and France.

The trade was carried on all over England. People were used to working at it and talking about it. At York in the North there is still the fifteenth-century chapel and hall of the Merchant Adventurers. (They sold cloth; the Merchants of the Staple sold the wool.) Halls of the mercers, their exchanges and storage depots and queys for export to Antwerp, Ghent, and Calais were usual in towns and not uncommon in the villages. Over England were churches built from the wool trade (Norfolk had most), and the great houses of the wool merchants. At Coggeshall, in Essex, is the house of Thomas Paycock, clothier in the 1400's, and in the small stone-built Cotswold village of Chipping Campden, thirty-five miles northwest of Oxford, on its beautiful medieval street, is the house that William Grevel built—"late citizen of London, and flower of the wool merchants"—and the church where he was buried.

The trade brought wealth to nobles who had land, and great wealth to many English merchants; by increasing their incomes, it made yeoman farmers more independent and strong, and gave freer choice and action to stewards, factors, clerks, business agents, and men with small businesses—the intelligent middle class; and it lessened the poverty of the very poor. (It had the doubtful good, which one writer praised, that children, "come to be sixe or seun yeares of age . . . were able to get their owne bread.") It did much else, and for many others. It increased building and helped to make beautiful, by wealth, at least part of what was built; and it touched the lesser arts, and the schools; and it bettered the towns. It touched, that is, everyone. "It hath been, and yet is, the nourishing of many thousands. . . ."

This success and wonder brought England pride in the trade and a feeling for it close to affection. It deserved their pride, and was almost beyond it. Other nations, watching, suspected that the English were losing a decent humility to arrogance, and they generalized about English self-satisfaction. It was fair enough, they granted, to give the wool trade credit for the wealth and good living it brought, but England seemed sure that all this came to them because of their special, unique, English qualities (as, indeed, most of it did, though some credit might go to the qualities of English grass). The English, they said, sometimes gave their success in business a moral value. They were sure their great wool trade proved their virtues. So outsiders went on saying the English were complacent; and they made that an English trait.

Certainly, pride in the great trade was everywhere in England, though probably not always quite the kind of pride those others, outside of England, thought it. Such national and personal success was temptation to great self-satisfaction. At best, it was childlike. And it was smiled at and forgotten by those who loved the

English, and, largely, by later times; but it was an irritant in the 1400's to Scotsmen and the French, having for them no charm and innocence at all.

The English recognized the wide presence and power of the trade, and they expressed their success positively: the Lord Chancellor of England sat on a woolsack in the House of Lords. And, too, the nation and the time idealized the trade, which they felt was especially theirs. Thomas Deloney, a writer and a weaver, born it seems at Norwich, praised his craft and the men who had worked at the looms as he had. He dedicated his novels—vivid, romantic, fast-moving, factual records of the clothmaker's life—to "the famous cloth-makers of England," in hope, he said, that the books would "raise out of the dust of forgetfulness [the memory of] most famous and worthy" men. Deloney was sure the weavers deserved "to be both loved and maintained," for "Among all Crafts this was the onely chiefe, for that it was the greatest merchandize, by the which our Countrey became famous through all Nations."

Thou Shalt Labor Till
Thou Retvrne To Dvst

Deloney put this motto on two of his title pages. He seems to have held it as a promise.

Field Festivals

To write of May Day in London, or of Midsummer Eve there, may seem wandering far afield from nationalism; pleasant perhaps but not touching the center. Yet such London holidays show, truly and humanly, that the great city was close to other parts of England and they to it. Such holidays and festivals may prove this as surely as analysis does or listed facts, and may suggest how warm and strong the bonds were. They may show, too, that English nationalism rested more on inherent qualities than even on geography and political needs. Indeed, in English fields, different as they were, and in the winds and skies and rivers and hills and moors, and in the ocean lie much that explains the unity of England.

The men of the 1400's seem to have been strongly affected by the places they grew up in, by the physical world around them, the town or country familiar and close. As a whole, they liked their homes, and from this liking flowed (because it rose out of experience and feeling) a companionship with others born and bred in England.

England was not so large that great distance divided it. It was fifty-one thousand square miles in extent without Scotland or Wales; about one-fourth the size of France; a little larger than the state of New York or of Pennsylvania; less than one-third the size of California. It was a small half-island, no part over two hundred fifty miles from any other, or more than seventy miles from the sea. And the sea winds were strong.

A turn of phrase from the place he had grown up in, old familiar sights and smells and customs—personal unimportant matters, really, that belonged only to him—joined one Englishman to another. For their living, though different, had likeness in its acts and its meaning. Their personal experiences, so unlike yet so like, could give different men common pleasures on happy, usual days, and might bring them to common action when that was needed.

* * * * *

On May Day morning, "from old time," London "every year set up [a] May Pole. . . . In the midst of the street before the south side of" St. Andrew Undershaft—"the fair and beautiful church in Cornhill," John Stow wrote. (His tomb is in St. Andrew.) The pole, or "shaft," was hung with pennons and swinging garlands and ribbons, and—if an old print is true—it rose above the six-storey houses around it and above the weathercock on the church spire. *"At-Shaft* or *Undershaft* was given to St. Andrew during the fifteenth century, when the Maypole was set up by it each May Day." And on May Day morning early, by three o'clock, crowds from London went into the fields to bathe their faces with the dew on the grass. Two centuries later, May Day morning, Elizabeth Pepys went into the fields in her coach, and Pepys was "troubled for fear of any hurt happening to her."

In "June and July, on the vigils [the eves] of festival days, and on the same festival days in the evening after the sun setting," Londoners, time out of mind, made bonfires in the streets (as countrymen did in the villages), "every man bestowing wood and labour towards them." The wealthy set up tables "with sweet bread and good drink . . . plentiful"; and "they would invite their neighbours and passangers also to sit and be merry with them in great familiarity, praising God for his benefits bestowed." The fires were called *bonfires,* Stow explains, because of "good amity among neighbours . . . controversy reconciled, and . . . bitter enemies [become] loving friends; and also for the virtue that a great fire hath to purge the infection of the air."

One evening of June was the festival of the Marching Bands, the volunteer police of London, two thousand "old soldiers of skill, meet for princes' use," who marched three miles or so through the City. To light them, seven hundred men carried cressets on long staves—iron bowls with oil or pitch pine blazing in them. With the Marching Bands was music—drums, fifes, horns, kettle-drums, and the trumpeters on horseback. Mixed into this show of light and motion and music and color were minstrels, Morris dancers, and the Waits of London to sing and play.

Such London holidays were London shows, but in their spirit and even in their form they were very much the country's. Surely, a countryman, if a little overwhelmed, would have felt at home in these festivals, and a Londoner would have found familiarity in a Yorkshire or a Devon Midsummer Eve.

On the eve of St. John the Baptist, whose day was June 24, and of St. Peter and St. Paul, whose days were June 29 and 30, "every man's door" (This seems to have been most in the center of the town near the Thames, the most crowded part.) was "shadowed with green birch, long fennel, St. John's wort, orpin, white lilies, and such like." And "lamps of glass, with oil burning in them all the night" were set at the doors—"hundreds of lamps alight at once, which made a goodly show."

The flowers and herbs and branches above the doors were com-mon country growths, easily found in the fields or by a brook over most of England in summer. Orpin—*sedum*—was a low-growing, creeping plant with small fleshy leaves and small yellow flowers in clusters; a weed so hardy that, uncontrolled, it could choke out a garden. It was sometimes called *live-forever*. It had little value. St.-John's-wort was another weed, mosslike, vivid green with massed small yellow flowers. It killed the good grass. Only goats could safely eat it. Fennel grew tall and strong and had bright yellow blossoms. Its roots could be "boiled in broths and drinks," and its seeds might season pickles and fruits and pippin pies. It had "great use to trim up, and strew upon fish." Out of control, it would overrun a garden or a field. These were the *facts* of the field.

But behind the choice of these herbs and grasses for the doorway was more than their field qualities. Each had present *beauty* of color: the birch was silver-gray and pale green; orpin and fennel and St.-John's-wort had gold-colored blossoms and green leaves; lilies were unsurpassably white. And white, and clear yellow, and green were spring colors, and holy colors.

And—very important in the choosing—each plant had about it a *legend;* a Christmas one or the memory of some ancient magic that reached back into pagan times. The birch had been a sacred tree for the Druids before English history began. In later belief ghosts who returned carried a branch of it or wore it, as the three sons did in *Usher's Well.* St.-John's-wort was, in the Norse sagas, the flower of Balder the Sun God, who died at the winter solstice—midwinter, the time of year opposite Easter—and who came back again, and whose day became, for Christians, St. John the Evangelist's Day, the twenty-seventh of December. St.-John's-wort—*erbe Ion,* in the form of the time—kept evil spirits from entering the doorways it shadowed. It could be worn as a charm. It warded off thunderbolts and melancholy. But cattle and horses with any white in their coats had best not eat it. One name for it was devil chaser—*fuga demonorum.* Fennel had strong power to clear a man's sight; to "take away the web or film that dimmeth our eyes." Lilies had pagan and Christian meanings. Lilies were the sign of a new power and purity, and of the old, perpetual renewing of life.

All England knew these facts and implications. It may not be too much to say that, like the garlands over the doors, these festivals (which had in them action and good fun, kindness, simplicity, beauty of form and colors, old meaning and memory, old myths and traditions, and which belonged in the villages and set townspeople thinking of the country) expressed and strengthened and confirmed the unity of England.

4

A NOTE ON PRICES

The Norfolk *Books*[1] are, all through, account books. In them a steward of the Duke set down, day by day, without comment, what he paid out for the household and what he took in. On each page—five hundred twenty as they are printed—is posted a column of items. These items, the cost of things five hundred years ago, are strange—startling—today.

Common services, and goods in common use, were cheap. A laborer, for instance, got ij.d., two pence a day: four American cents at the old ratio (used here) of five dollars to a pound; in present English currency, about half that. A month's pay to a kitchen woman was thirty-two cents. A skilled carpenter got eight cents a day. A plumber's bill "for mending of the pippe lede" came to eight cents. Commonly, the cost of a shave was two cents, but "Fynche, for shavying my Lord" got eighteen cents. "My Lordes dyner" on a journey was fifteen pence, and "His souper, xxij.d." Once the Duke paid the barber only eight cents.

Wheat was, usually, 5s.8d. a *quarter*—eight bushels. Two chickens were four cents; a goose, eight cents (but a goose-feather bed was thirty-two shillings). A lamb was eight cents; a hundred eggs, twelve cents; a quart of wine, two cents. A common horse went at four shillings; a "troting nagge" at ten shillings. "A grey nage to send to the French King" cost thirty-five shillings, but his shoeing was only a penny.

For "Tom fole is cheys [his shoes]" twelve cents was paid. The Duke kept two fools: Richard, the other, graded lower than Tom.

---

[1] *Household Books of John Duke of Norfolk and Thomas Earl of Surrey;* 1481-1490; J. Payne Collier, Editor; Roxburghe Club; 1844.

He was "the fool of the kitchen." Next after a gift to the Abbey of Bury St. Edmonds stands, in happy contrast, "Item, to the fole of the said place, iiij.d." Sir John the priest, "for syngyng messe," had regularly eight cents, and "the friar that heard the Duke's confession" was given forty-two cents.

Norfolk, as he left the castle of his son, Thomas Earl of Surrey, gave twenty-two cents for distribution "to the pore-folke at the gate." (Two hundred years later, Samuel Pepys wrote with satisfaction that when he left Cambridge in his carriage, "the poor . . . did stand at the coach to have something given them, as they do to all great persons; and I did give them something." October 7, 1667.) Four cents was no meagre offering to a church, nor was a penny—two cents—thin alms to a poor man or an empty gift to a child.

Such expenses of the Duke's were level with those of any other landlord, but he was, too, from his position, in a world of vastly different costs. For one thing, he must, by the custom of his rank, reward well all services done him, and must give with special liberality to the servants in a noble household; and he must leave liberal alms at great shrines and great churches. Two pence might be right enough for an ordinary wandering minstrel when his singing was done (and be most thankfully taken), but five shillings, twenty-five times the other gift, went "to my Lord of Gloucesters" minstrels. The usual and liberal gift of, say, twenty-four cents "to a Palmer" on pilgrimage to the Holy Land, or of eight cents to the friars of Colchester Abbey was of necessity strengthened by the Duke to twenty shillings at the great shrine of Our Lady of Walsingham.

So, too, for their special goods—clothing is an example—the nobles paid high prices. Enough black silk for the Duke's doublet, at nine shillings a yard, cost twenty-two shillings. "Cremysyn satin" for a doublet came to twenty shillings. A yard of black velvet—"velewet blake"—was fifteen shillings; purple velvet was sixteen shillings. "Gold upon damask" cloth rose to four pounds, six shillings, and eight pence a yard.

Blue damask for a hood came to three and a half shillings, but the hoodmaker's pay was sixteen cents. The maker of the Duke's black satin doublet got thirty-two cents. A hat for the steward ("for myself," he wrote into the account) cost ten cents. The Duke's great gift to the Lord Protector, Richard of Gloucester, was a cup of gold with a cover, that weighed five pounds and a half. A "potte" for cooking came to a penny.

This difference in the costs of the gold cup and the cooking pot is not unfair in its implications. The *Books* repeat such separation on, literally, every page of the accounts. The 1400's never supposed there was (or could be) a ratio between "noble expenditures" and a laborer's needs. To all concerned such comparison lay outside the order of nature.

Equally, even to approximate a fixed ratio between our money and the money of the Duke's accounts is baffling and seems—in the end—impossible. The cost of building Stratford Latin School in 1426-27 was set down at the time as £9 17s.11½d.; the Provost of Jesus College in Yorkshire (1483) was to be paid—liberally—£13 6s.5d. a year, and a teacher there got £5 6s.8d.; a lord chief justice in London got £120, and a country priest had £6 a year in money. All these men had lodgings and "robes" and unnamed fees and the expected gifts.

In 1865 Dr. Charles Knight wrote, "Multiply these [fifteenth-century] values by fifteen for present money-value." In 1915 Professor A. P. Leach wrote that the income of Eton College in 1441 (about £660) was equal "to at least £20,000 now"; that is, to a hundred thousand dollars. In 1957 Professor A. L. Rowse wrote that a pound in 1600 bought twenty times what it bought in 1957.

Such different values seem to come out of quite different monetary worlds, as indeed they do. Put into arithmetic, such relations stand fantastic and impossible.

It is, of course, possible to set side by side the price of wheat five hundred years ago and now. That gets an exact ratio. The comparison of such a clear-cut, commonly-used object gives the fact and suggests, too, the immensity of difference which time has brought. Yet it is an isolated, limited comparison; and so, sets a ratio that is artificial and untrue. A less exact measuring, one made from many objects and kept within the 1400's, would more nearly show the truth.

5

MUSIC

The isle is full of noises,
Sounds and sweet airs that give delight...
Tempest

"Noble Music"

English music in the 1400's was the best music in Europe. On
the Continent, by 1450, the English school was held "the 'fount
and origin' of what virtually was a new art [*ars nova esse videatur
... spud Anglicos*], so wonderfully did it surpass previous music."
So it was said in Flanders, Bologna, Rome. They realized this
rather more than England did, then much taken up with its wars
at home and in France.

John Dunstable (He died in 1453.) gave England this surpassing
position. He was the great—the unapproachable—musician and, as
the time put it, *mathematician*. Today, the sixty or so pieces by
him, or said to be by him, prove his deserved rank. Sir John Squire
wrote, "Not only [was he] the first of all great English composers
... but he was as powerful in Europe as Purcell was later"—about
1680. King Henry VI seems to have been his "patron, friend, and
collaborator."

Many in the century gave this highest praise to English music.
A German nobleman about 1470, after he had heard the choir of
Edward IV at the Chapel Royal in London, wrote, "There are no
better singers in the world." A French doctor of the time, "though
envious and spiteful" of most he found in England, wrote: "The
English are joyous one with another and they greatly love music."
A Fleming ("Tinctoris, the celebrated ... theoretician" of music)
placed English music above compare. Erasmus (educated in the

last half of the 1400's) wrote, "The English may claim to be . . . the most musical of people." Out of the bright age of Elizabeth, Sir Philip Sidney, looking back, confessed that the old music stirred his heart more than a trumpet.

This is the standing which the classical music of England, "noble music," had in Europe in the fifteenth century.

Popular Music

Fifteenth-century England sang in season and out of season, or rather every season was the time to sing. This England never was a nest of singing birds; but it made music a constant, easy companion. People were at home with music. They liked to hear the sounds of instruments and singing about them. Music was everywhere—an unforced, unhindering, native way of speech. Indeed, it seems to have been to them rather like the sunlight which was on and around each visible object, giving it form and colors.

It may be right for the time that Chaucer's pilgrims, all of them—knight, prioress, parson, plowman, lawyer, doctor, Oxford scholar—were shepherded out of London on the Canterbury road with bagpipe tunes, played by the miller.

* * * * *

With a readiness hard to realize the people of the 1400's turned their moods and memories and hopes and actions directly into music—into lyrics, and narrative ballads, and songs for dancing, and twenty other forms. For one thing they sang when they were happy. In day-by-day England, as truly as in a painted country of romance, people were singing from pure pleasure, under the stir of gaiety, and in warm satisfaction. The feeling did not need to be strong. Strangers ferrying across the Thames might sing in fellowship, if they liked their company. ("I," said one of the four men at a country inn, "will sing a song if anybody will sing another." "I promise you I will sing," the shepherd answered. "What will you sing?" asked the first.)

The welcome at lodgings or at a friend's house might be a song, and a song and a kiss from the hostess and the host might be goodbye. In 1466 a German noble travelling with company in England was astonished when he found the hostess of an inn "come into the street to receive them all with her household, singing; and they all kissed." Working or at leisure, they sang old jigs and glees, a political jingle, a nursery rhyme, a new tune bought from a wandering packman, a Church memory. Some of them, isolated at home—perhaps weaving—might sing, half-absently in pleasant sadness, a tragic ballad, or a tale of "disprised love"—an "old and antique song" such as Shakespeare's Duke Orsino asked for, "which dallies with the innocence of love/ Like the Old Age."

They sang, too, because others were singing. Singing was around them, a pleasant contagion. To follow music was to follow the time, to share sun and rain. They heard—repeated through all their life—the music of the Church: the bells at every hour in country and town (London had almost a hundred sounding steeples); often, the Mass and the innocence of a village choir; and, possibly, once or twice, Edward IV's astonishingly perfect choir. At home they made music, and in every school, and they used it out of doors in the streets for gaiety or salesmanship. They were part of it at fairs and festivals (which came more often than they do now), and at coronations and royal christenings and royal marriages, and after a notable victory; in all of which they had their part. The Cycles the guilds put on had gusty songs in them—hearty, local fun; and they had in them a few touching songs, such as Mary's lullaby in the *Townley Plays*. (From 1200 to 1900 songs were part of English plays. Now, in or out of plays, the time does not sing at all.)

So, lawyers at their Inns; and shepherds ("Your shepherd is an honest man; let him sing."); and merchants, and lovers, and raw apprentices; Oxford students, soldiers, children, the king—were singing. Alone or together, poor or rich, happy or dull or miserable, they found occupation or relief or happiness in a song; and they were sure to find companionship in it. Music even gave to some boys who had good singing voices and good minds for study, a way out into wide success. It did, for instance, to Richard Pace, at the Church School in Winchester, when he was nine or ten years old.

The coarsest had their vulgarities, their satisfying, meaty songs, which, for taste, were level with cheap comics and the hundred best tunes of the week. Some rhymings told, too, political libels or the agony of callow and budding love ("a song ballad for dairy-wenches"); or it repeated stock jokes on women and marriage (ballads of old men with young wives, or of *The Hard-Hearted Maid*, or, vice-versa, of *Two Maids Wooing a Man*— "This in request I can tell you.") Some of them carried in their jingle-jangle salty jokes for "stretch-mouthed rascals." All of them are cheap in tune and in substance, and easy to get the point of. By any fair estimate most of them were "jogging rhymes set to a vile tune and sung by a worse voice." Such songs drifted down over England like blown pollen; songs which many took, and sang for a while, and forgot.

(The learned antiquarian and lawyer John Selden held that "the more solid . . . the more excellent and well-turned songs . . . do not show the times as well as ballads and libels" do, though the doggerals be "a most false gallop of verses." Those of the 1400's do show a wide, crude surface of the times.)

People sang and listened from many other impulses, for music fitted all the dimensions of their lives. It brought to them interesting goings-on—a murder, the war in France, politics ("what the lawyers are up to"), a fist fight, a pelican, a talking dog, the birth and wonder of a phoenix, scandals and fashions at Court, floods and fires and prices of corn, the old Bible story of Constant Susannah. Ballads told how to catch fish and when to sow the grain, and the cure for a sick cow. And by their tunes and rhyming they helped a man remember his alphabet and his counting, or something else he wanted to keep in his mind. The point is that in hundreds of ways the people—all sorts of people—got fun, and use, and romance out of their songs.

Of course, no one sang all the time, as some writing may suggest. No one did "go to church in a galliard and come in a coranto," and make his very walk a jig. As a whole, though, the years were happy and alive with music.

Some got no pleasure from it. The men and women who wrote the *Paston Letters* do not tell they sang or ever listened to singing with pleasure. Some direct-minded people saw only the black and white visibility of prose. They—admirable or otherwise—lived untouched by the music which was strong and warm about them.

For all about them others were singing out of uncountable impulses; and the intensity of their impulses varied from a flooding tide of feeling to the useful, singsong purpose of learning the ABC's. In the 1400's music was a natural speech.

Country Songs

Though it is easy to separate country songs and London songs, the separation is artificial. Largely, all England sang the same songs. Country and town, because their ways were different, each was bound to have songs drawn from its own ways, but the division did not get much below the surface, below the subject, the topic of the verse. And it is to be remembered that the English, London-bred or not, were a rural people.

Most liked a song—old or new—which was alive, fresh, direct, emotional, a pleasure to their ears and their tastes wherever it had been made; and they held to tradition. That gave a wide sweep to their interests, and brought them popular music of many sorts. So, along with reaping and milking and hunting songs—country songs —they all sang London street songs, if they liked that sort, and ballads of city people and city happenings, and traditional carols, and what-not old and new. They sang of silver streams and the greenwood, and romantic haymaking; and, equally, of Dick Whittington, and the love of *A London Maid*. They all liked such songs, and they liked, too, songs of border wars and foreign wars, and songs of love—happy or unhappy, of spring, youth, courtship and the marriage-to-come, not thinking whether the song was urban or unurban, North or South, telling of a London apprentice or a shepherd. Most of these popular ballads were crudely done. A very few were fresh, delightful, true music; and beautiful by their art or their seeming artlessness.

These popular songs had in them what their makers and their singers liked to think of and see and do. One thing they liked was the country—land and sky and water, and the products of the land. The English lived close to the country when they could, and wherever they were they made gardens for colors and smells and use: costly gardens to give green spaces and knotted flower beds and bordered walks and pools and mazes of clipped yew; and simple gardens that had in them fruit and vegetables and herbs. They used many herbs. Formal pleasances and walled kitchen gardens pleased them. So did a cottage garden with the local flowers and some fruit trees, or with berry bushes and rows of vegetables, and vines. All these got into their songs.

They told in their songs what went on outside the parks and gardens and towns—in the fields, the woods, the untilled pasturing, the sky. They watched the land and the seasons. In early summer, when the woods still were fresh with the new sap, before late June, the leaves were "large and long." Red sky at morning was the shepherd's warning. By April rabbits were alert in the barren land; and cuckoos called in early spring, and nightingales sang, then, "to welcome in the spring." Country songs told a hundred thousand such matters, seen and felt.

Country songs were full of people. There were romantic outlaws; and young lovers, lost or made quite happy; and men and women struck by the fatality of war or sickness or treachery, or caught into some mysterious, raw, household tragedy—a mother whose three dead sons come home to her from the churchyard on a November night; a son whose blade drips with his father's blood; a lover poisoned (with eels) by his lady. We know these old tales

69

from the ballads of two hundred years later; from *The Wife of Usher's Well, Edward* ("Why does your blade so drip with blood, Edward?"), *Lord Randell,* and *Barbara Allen,* which in 1666 Samuel Pepys listened to "in perfect content."

There were factual country songs, the realities of local happenings. They told of April rain drowning all the fields; of ducking the village scold in the pond; of the King's visit; of a suicide by hanging and his ghost truly seen; of plague close by; of fires and storms. These were, most of them, poor limping stuff, as was natural, and they are well lost; yet now and then—but rarely—by happy circumstance a song took lovely shape and is still known.

This does not mean they romanticized the country. Fifteenth-century men knew the practical side of farming — fertilizing (Chaucer had written of that), draining, plowing, and harrowing, the care of sheep, and other matters they needed to know. They studied these, and thought them over. But they did not put them into song. They might be touched into rhyming two lines of hope about their spring plowing ("God speed the plough,/And send us corn enough"), but that was another matter.

London Songs

London did have its own songs. There were, for instance, those the London Waits sang. The Waits, at first, were the watchmen who played their trumpets, or sang as they called the night hours and did their mild policing or as they went off duty. By the 1400's they had become a company of professional musicians, in part supported by the City for its pageants and civic ceremonies. The group had occupation all year round, and for excellence and interest to Londoners, reached up toward the Choir of the Chapel Royal, and "my Lord of Gloucester's trumpeters" in the 1480's.

The Waits of London were the best there were, but every parish in town or country "had its resident musicians, called Waits." Since there was hardly a sport or a festival that did not have music as part of it, the Waits found plenty of employment. The festivals went on from Whitsuntide, the seventh Sunday after Easter (say, early June), through Lammas day, August first, and Harvest Home ("which brought its separate festivals from farm to farm") and into Christmas time and Twelfth Night, and even on to Easter.

Besides this music for leisure and celebration London had its business songs, the street songs; probably unlovely most of them, more noise than music, but not always so. Yet the chance of hearing melody in the street hubbub was a poor give-and-take of—with luck—perhaps twenty to one. At any rate, Londoners heard many songs that belonged to their town, and were singing many.

Some in the town had to sing. They earned their living that way. They did sing for their suppers. Each trade, each kind of wandering street-seller, had a special selling-song, his vendor's rhythm and cry. A muffin-man with his tray sang his own advertisement, and he had to sing his muffin-praise loud against the competing uproar of the street. A fish-seller had his catch, a strawberry-girl hers, and so had the woman with country flowers or fresh milk, and the seller of flash trinkets or of a newly-written ballad. The lavender-woman had a song curious and pleasant, handed down from mother to child. It sometimes was sung in two parts, one voice answering another across the narrow street. Apprentices by their master's shop bawled out their selling tune; and since a shop-front might be only fifteen feet or so wide, the dissonance was strong and steady.

The list of popular ballads native to London is short. London had few songs which were quite its own, limited to it by substance. Mostly, the songs London sang were those sung all over England. Even into the roar of, say, Thames Street and Cheapside and the wards by the Bridge, came, strongly, songs unpointed by special city topic. Such general songs sounded in London taverns and barbershops—signs of fellowship, or a way to pass the time of waiting. A lute lay on the barber's table. Singing was as usual as looking at picture pages is today. Boatmen ferrying the Thames sang any sort of English song. A cobbler's shop of the time, with its young journeymen shoemakers, "seemed," wrote Thomas Deloney later in his *Raven's Almanac,* "a verrie bird-cage."

Household Music of John Howard

The *Household Books* of John Howard (1430-1485), made Duke of Norfolk by Richard III in June, 1485, tell the kind of music he had with him at his manor of Stoke Nayland, about fifty miles northeast of London, in Essex, while he was there from February, 1481, to March, 1485. The Duke, then, was in his middle fifties.

Norfolk, whom Shakespeare wrote of in *Richard III,* was powerful in England for thirty years—Knight of the Garter, Treasurer, Admiral, Member of Parliament, Constable of the Tower, Earl Marshall, envoy to Louis XI and to Burgundy, a noble fighter by land and sea against the French, the Hanseatic League, the Scotch in special, and always against the Lancastrians. He was "a very pollityke and skillful in warres," wrote Polydore Vergil. He died with Richard at Bosworth, in the early morning ("Stir with the lark tomorrow, gentle Norfolk!"), leading the "vanward" of the King's army. In the front line of battle "wer placyed his [Richard's] archers, lyke a most strong trenche and bulward; of these archers, he made . . . leder, John duke of Norfolk."

The Duke delighted in many sorts of music. He had the greatest pleasure in the flow and counterpoise and lovely solution of a melody. And he had much pleasure in the lesser music, the general and common kinds: the comfortable, honest drone of a bagpipe, gay leaping English jigs, the broad jocularities brought by bands of singers and juggler-minstrels, who wandered the road most seasons, after the custom of the times. When he went up to London, he had the Waits to sing before him and the City trumpeters to play. His account books show this.

Music is often an item in the *Books*. Gifts to musicians are set down: "Item, to a mynstrell xx.d."; and money to the Earl of Kent's minstrels, to my lord of Buckingham's, and to others. Trumpeters are named, and taborers, and a piper, and often harpplayers.

The Duke dealt well by harpers. He liked them. A gray gown, made from four "yerds of narowe cloth," went to "Thomas the Herperd." It must have been a good gown, for it was expensive. It cost the Duke five shillings and eight pence. Thomas the Harper was part of the household. There were besides, "an arper that played before by Lord" and got forty cents, and "an nother harpper, who played the same day." At his manor, October 18, 1482, the Duke, four or five months home from his good victory in Scotland, "made covenant with Will'm Wastell, of London, harper, that he should have the son of John Colet, of Colchester, harper, for a yere, to teche him to harpe and synge, for the whiche techynge my Lord shall give him xiiij.s.iiij.d. and a gown." As earnest money, to bind the bargain, the Duke that day gave William six shillings and four pence, and promised again, at the end of the year, to give him "the Remenaunt, and is [his] gowne."

The Duke had at least one man singer in his household, and at different times three or four or five Children of the Chapel Choir—singing boys whom he supported, and educated in music and other needed arts. Their names show in the accounts—"grete Dyke, Edward, and Harry . . . of the Chapel." They are named more than once. So, too, is "litel Richard, synger."

Easter Day, 1484, each of the boys was given new shoes or had his old ones "clowtyn"—mended. Shoes (by pleasant variation of spelling *choys, shoys, shoes, choys, schoyes)* come often to be paid for at, usually, 5d.; and the accounts credit the Duke with assiduously supplying these boys with "hosen." Often, four cents is put down for the mending of these: "Item, to Robyn of the Stabell for mending of his hoseyn ij.d."

At Stoke were many kinds of instruments—drums large and small, pipes and trumpets, "serpents," fiddles, lutes, bagpipes, shalms (oboe-like reed instruments), organs. In the chapel was an organ, and there may have been another for the Duchess. For the mending of a lute, a minstrel was paid two shillings and four pence. A flow of music, by voices and instruments, seems to have been constant when Norfolk was at Stoke Nayland.

There were others like the Duke, generous in appreciation and support. Among the many were Humphrey of Gloucester (whatever his large faults) and, in special, Anthony Woodville, Lord Rivers, and the Lady Margaret Beaufort. All English kings and queens in the century maintained, as part of the royal responsibility, singers and instrument-players, whom they took with them wherever their Household went in war or peace.

The Peoples' Language

To discuss fifteenth-century music is, sometimes, to get away from it; to go the long way home. Music was the people—the one person who wrote and the others who sang or heard. Music could be only what they were. Its origin and substance and structure of tones came from them. Music was the speech of a person and a people and a time; each of which had profound uniqueness, and unity with the others, and a constant shift and change of surface.

Music did not exist in the 1400's as "an isolated function of sound" (if an isolated function ever does exist) because it would have had nothing to say. It would have had no substance at all.

Music rises into existence out of someone's acts and thoughts and feelings. It is his substance, made from his living. What had made him, made his music. So, to write of anything about fifteenth-century England is, in its way, to write about music.

Music—so close and strong an expression of the century—gained strength and extent as language and business and government gained. It gained unity as England was unified. It gained by all other gains—by printing, for instance, which helped bring into use one system of musical notation; one way of writing the sounds of a song. And music gained and spread because people expected most poetry to be sung. No one then questioned this union of poetry and

73

singing—an interdependence which went on ("the unsurpassed marriage of music and words") into the 1700's. For five hundred years not much music was heard that did not get words set to it. A poet expected his poem to find its tune; and every tune would find its verses.

6

SCHOOLS

Noble Education

1.

Young nobles, like other boys, were a mixed lot. In qualities and training they made up a scattered field. Some had a wide and humane education, as Chaucer's *Squire* had about 1380, or Edward IV in the middle of the 1400's. The *Squire's* training followed the fashion of his time and rank. He learned his languages and his logic; the ideals and manners of knighthood; the use of arms. He learned to sing and make songs, to play the flute, to dance, and he was modest, diligent, fought well in Flanders, served his father the *Knight,* and enjoyed the spring. Edward IV, after he became, unsteadily, king at nineteen in 1461, had *Livy* and *Josephus* and his Bible finely bound; he gave Caxton in 1479 £20, a good sum; of his letter in French to Louis XI in 1475, Commines, the King's councilor, said, "I could scarcely believe an Englishman wrote it"; and he was the handsomest, most courteous young prince in Europe, and the best in fighting, and brilliant in the arts. "He was of visage lovely, of body mighty, strong"; and his height measured six feet three inches and a half.

Some young English nobles were trained only in hunting and fighting. "By God's body, I had rather that my son should hang than study Latin!" said one noble. "For it becomes the sons of gentlemen to blow the hunting-horn well, to hunt skillfully, and elegantly to carry and train the hawk." A gentleman was to be a gentleman, and no nonsense about it. Education touched only a part of the nobility.

Some boys of great families were educated not in schools or at home, but in the household of the King or of a high official. A boy who had served well the Lord Chancellor or the Duke of Norfolk was assured that later he would get his splendid chance. It was the most direct, perfect training imaginable for its end. The boy had part, day after day, in the activities of peace and war usual for a feudal lord. And in the rare, glittering visits of Warwick—the King's officer and the highest noble in England—to his castle, he saw proof both of the glory he might rise into and of its practical, measurable gains. This sort of education was not common. It was difficult to enter, and it was expensive, and it was a hard test.

The education of a royal child and of *"enfans des famille,* children of good houses," was carefully planned. Their Governor was directed "to show [them] the urbanity and nurture of England, to learn them to ride cleanly and surely," to make certain that they had skill in arms (for arms was a very great part of all this) and that they used "all courtesy in word [and] deeds." He should eat with them "in the hall . . . at the same board" so that "mannerly they do ete and drinke . . . after the book of courtesy." When necessary, he was to use the stick.

Even to the small boys music was to be studied "for delight." It was to be an easement and encourager to them under the heavy burdens of their other study. So part of the day was spent on singing and on "pastimes of instruments . . . upon the lute and virginalls." Music of course never would be the happy spontaneous employment to them that sport was: "For his recreation [a boy] useth to hawke and hunte, and shote in his long bowe . . . which [a young boy] seemeth to be thereunto given by nature."

Older, at seventeen or eighteen, as squires, these boys were "wynter and sumer, in aftyrnoones and in evenings, to drawe to [their] lordes chambres within courte, there to kepe honest company . . . in talking of cronycles of Kings and of polycyes, or in pypeyng or harpyng or synging," or in feats of arms, which were "to help occupy [entertain] the courte." They were, too, to stay with strangers at Court and talk with them until "tyme require [the guests'] departing." One fact is sure: for these young nobles, skill in arms, in music, in courtesy and manners, ability to carve at the table, and even to make verses, were more important than their Latin or philosophy. Chaucer's young *Squire* had much this training in the 1300's.

So, too, in the middle 1400's had Richard of Gloucester, the youngest brother of Edward IV. From nine years to thirteen or fourteen years (April, 1461 to November, 1465) Richard of Gloucester was a page at the Earl of Warwick's magnificent and crowded castle, Middleham Castle, three hundred years old, in north Yorkshire. For that "time of maintenance" away from home the King paid Warwick £1,000.

A day of this training, in a generalized sequence which is not the routine of any one day, went like this: Morning—early Mass at six; bread and meat and wine; study of some Latin and more French and a little law and mathematics and logic and music and penmanship, and very much study of the spirit and rules of chivalry. Afternoon—dinner, the chief meal, soon after nine-thirty; then, outside the castle until four in summer, jousting on horseback at a quintain or at the rings, hawking sometimes, or sometimes riding in armor and fighting with blunted weapons, or practicing on foot with a blunted sword and buckler or with a battle-axe or daggers, running and leaping and wrestling and casting heavy bars and throwing spears; then, in the castle again at four or five, meat and bread and wine or ale. After the meal the pages engaged in "the polite arts of singing, harping, playing the lute, dancing" and courtly talk with ladies of the castle; and they would "oftimes . . . in the countess's bower . . . [play] all chamber-games—chess, and backgammon, and dice." At the end came the ale and bread, and then sleep in more or less one common hall. Privacy was the luxury for a later age. The boys at six or seven already could read Latin or French and the English of the Court. They probably always read aloud.

The Household Book of the Duke of Northumberland, in 1500, shows this same routine: Mass at six, dinner at half-past nine or ten, supper at four, "gates all shut at nine; no ingress or egress permitted."

For the education of his first son, Edward IV drew up full directions when the Prince was a baby. Prince Edward was born in November, 1470, as the civil war was running against his father. By May, Edward IV was fully king. Then he created his son, six months old, Prince of Wales, and set up for him a great establishment, complete with governor, chaplain, treasurer, nurse, and even a butcher, John Good. (This may be John Gould, the generous butcher, who at the time the Prince was born in the sanctuary of Westminster Abbey, where his mother had taken refuge from Henry VI, gave the Queen credit "for half a beef and two muttons every week." In sanctuary starvation might be a greater danger than capture.)

When the Prince was three, the King gave him a larger house-hold; appointed as his Governor his uncle Earl Rivers, a shining figure in war, at Court, and in the arts (his *Dictes or Sayings of the Philosophers* was the first book Caxton printed in England); made the Bishop of Rochester his tutor; drew up a full set of ordinances for "the virtuous guiding of the young child and for the good rule of his household"; and sent the Prince to Ludlow Castle on the Welsh border (possibly for safety), where he himself had been a young learner twenty years before.

Under the ordinances the Prince was to pass his day like this: (Ordinance 1) He was to rise early, have Matins sung by two chap-lains, and go to Mass—at about six o'clock. (2) On a holiday he was to "hear divine service" and (3) on principal fast days have sermons preached before him—at three years. (4) After Mass and a sermon he should eat his first meal, a light one, probably the inevitable ale or wine and meat and bread, study an hour (at a subject not named) "until he go to meat"—to dinner—about ten, at which his dishes were "to be borne by worshipful folk in our livery." (5) Later, he was to have "read before him, noble stories as behooveth a prince to understand, and allways all the talk in his presence [must be] of virtue, honour, cunning [learning], wisdom and deeds of wor-ship, [and] of nothing that shall move him to vice." (6) Next, so he should escape idleness, came two hours of study; and, after, "such [physical] disports and exercises [were] in his presence to be showed as belong to his estate." (7) The day ended for the Prince by his going "to evensong," (8) having a light supper (at four o'clock) and then "honest entertainment." (9) He was to be "in his chamber, and for all night, and the travers [curtains] to be drawn by nine of the clock, and all persones then . . . to be avoided"—shut out of the room. Ordinances 10 and 11 were that a "sure and good watch [was to be] nightly had and kept about his person for safeguard"; and that he was to be guarded in the daytime "from his rising to his going to bed." He was never to be alone. He was twelve, and at Ludlow, when he became king.

2.

A plan of education made a century later praises the noble edu-cation in the 1400's by using much of its plan. The great Lord Bacon's father, Sir Nicholas Bacon, then Attorney for the Court of Wards, which had oversight of young nobles under the guard-ianship of the crown, made out his plan "for bringing up [the noble wards] in virtue and learning." Sir Nicholas heartily disapproved the new sort of education the noble boys were getting, and he praised the older. The present education he thought "disgracefully negligent." So, first, he set down what should be the center of the ward's training. "The chiefe thinge, and most of price, . . . is his mynde; and next that, his bodie; and last and meanest, his land. Nowe, the chiefe care of governaunce hath bin to the land, the meaneste; [next] to the bodie . . .; but to the minde, being the best, none at all: Which methinkes is playnely to set the carte before the horse."

Then he gives his plan for bringing up the boys. Outlined, it is this: At six o'clock, "divine service" [nothing is said of a breakfast]; until eleven, Latin; eleven to twelve, dinner; twelve to two, music with a master; two to three, French; three to five, Latin and Greek; five to eight, prayer, supper, "honest recreations"; eight to nine, again music under a master; nine, bed. This training is close to Richard of Gloucester's at Middleham in the 1460's. So, a hundred years later it won the approval of a very wise man.

3.

Those in the 1400's who wrote about noble education gave high place in it to music. Always—and deeply—music was essential. Its value was accepted with no debate. Music, often named, was not often discussed. It lay, unquestioned, below the surface (which was talk of immediate aims and new ways) because it was part of the foundation. The unsettled and surface matters got most words.

The standing of music in education is proved by the times it is named in a boy's training or taken for granted. It runs through Richard III's day. Music comes as part of the six o'clock Mass; as a serious study along with Latin and mathematics and logic; as an overtone at the castle dinner; outdoors in the afternoon—in trumpets and clarions—as background of his training at arms. And alone or an accompaniment to talk and action, it colored the castle evening of "synging, harping, playing the fiddle, dancing and courtly talk."

It is surprising and interesting to find how strongly music does come into the boy's life. It could be to him a duty of his rank, a pure pleasure, a mathematical study, an accomplishment, a virtuous occupation, or praise to God. Always, it was part of the boy's day. For the "Muses, besides [being ladies of] learning, were also ladies of dancing, mirth, and minstrelsy; Apollo was god of shooting, and author of cunning playing upon instruments," wrote Roger Ascham.

79

Books of Courtesy

1.

Books of Courtesy were common in England in the fifteenth century. All had, or claimed to have, one aim—to teach boys (from eight or nine years to perhaps seventeen) what were courtly manners, and how noble and necessary such courtesy in action was; how fully it rested on religion, logic, and propriety. The books were in English, in verse—for easy remembering—and often were paraphrases out of Latin. They were no specialty of the century; they and their like stretch long before and long after the 1400's.

They were, some of them, by title, *The Boke of Curtasye* (1460), *Urbanitatis* (1460), *The Babees Book* (1475), *The Lytylle Childrenes Lytil Boke* (1480), *The Young Children's Book* (1500), *The Schoole of Virtue.*

These are as immeasurably apart in tone and value as those who wrote them were in experience, good sense, temperament, and character. Some of the authors were courtiers, men of special training and ability, and of special tastes. Their books are noble in tone, and definite. They show knowledge and authority and culture. Other books, it seems sure, for it is written broadly over them, were put together by persons who never had lived in a family of breeding, much less in a household where the spirit and practices of chivalry were inherent and were, too, directly taught. The lesser books set out a medley—crude and obvious, and not needed by a boy of sense and decent training. They got close to being a parody of noble education.

2.

The Babees Book is one of the best. It stands for the right sort. In it are thirty-one stanzas each of seven lines. The first eight stanzas, condensed, and in prose and modern spelling say this:

> May God support me (since I write not well) while I try to turn this Latin into our common tongue. My book shall teach those of tender age to know and use virtue and courteous ways.

> O children, adorned with grace and high birth, with beauty and ability, I call on you to know this book! For it were great pity that virtue and manners were not in you, so gifted as you are and of such sovereign beauty.

> Babes, my book is wholly for you. Don't wonder I write in verse. Men use it. ("Men ysen yt.") And if you don't know a word I use, ask till you get it, and then hold on to it ("holde yt in horde"—hold it among your treasure). So, by asking from wise men, you will learn.

And now I will tell you children who dwell in great households, how you should behave when you are set at table. In this aid me, O Mary Mother! And thou, Lady Wit, quicken my pen! Show thy help to me! This makes the first fifty-one lines.

The last stanza, lines 211 to 218, is, in the old spelling:

And, swete children, for whos love now I write,
I you beseche withe verrey lovande herte,
To knowe this book that yee sette your delyte.
And myhtefulle god, that suffred peynes smerte,
In curtesye he make you so experte,
That thurhe your nurture and your governaunce
In lastynge blysse yee mowe your self auaunce!

[That is: Sweet children, for whose love now I write, I, with loving heart, beseech you to know and to delight in this book. And may Almighty God, who suffered the pangs of pain, make you so courteous in your living that you shall attain unto eternal bliss.]

Clearly, the book was for well brought-up, intelligent boys; for the noble aspirants. It was for even royal children and for Pages of Honor (*Henxmen,* henchmen), whose service was close to the king or to the lord of the household. The third stanza speaks directly to

...yonge Babees, whome bloode Royalle
With grace, Feture, and hyhe habylite
Hathe enourmyd [endowed, adorned].

The books could well be a text for "younge gentylmen, Henxmen ...*Enfauntes*...as shall please the King."

Between the first stanza and the last the substance ranges from rules of behavior and maners, to religion; from clear speech and seemly eating, to the Mass and Aves and duty to the king and the immediate lord and to servants and the poor; from abhorrence of dirty fingers to purity of spirit.

The boy gets short, exact, rules, easy to remember:

No scratching; no crude sounds of eating; keep hands and knife and lips clean. After the meal, go up to the lord's table and pour the water on his hands, or hold the towel, or just wait to hear grace. Always go to early Mass, at 6. Be meek. Be cheerful. Be ready to bring drinks to your betters and hold lights for them. Don't throw bread at the table. Don't *ever* be late at a meal.

In one section of the book the aspirant is told exactly how to carry himself when he is summoned before his king or his lord. He is to walk into the room in a seemly way; kneel when close to his

81

lord, cap off; listen—attentively, chin up, eyes on his lord, no fidget-
ing—to what his lord is saying. When his lord is quite ended, he is
to answer in a clear tone, and directly and sensibly and concisely
(For many words be right tedious). After he is told to go, he is to
rise and leave in—again—a seemly way.

There are, to be sure, surprising, out-of-tone cautions against
crudeness not expected in such boys ("Don't scratch while you eat.
Don't pick your nose, or nails, or teeth."), but they get small space.
Usually the direction is solid, honest, needed. "Talk clearly, stand
straight, never fiddle your hands," he is told. "Always show courtesy to servants." "In youre fedynge [feeding] looke [to it that]
goodly yee be sene." Precept on precept, the boy is shown his fitting
service and its meaning.

The whole spirit of the book is right. Its kindly, urbane directions might have use today. For the boys are recognized as worth
teaching; they are worth consideration and interest. The writer
likes them. They are his "younge Babees" (*Babe,* then, meant
young and inexperienced; not as today), his "swete children,"
"bete [fair] Babees," boys of good blood, of grace and strength and
training and "high ability"—the selected he is sure; those worth
education, and needing it because of the postion and the duties
they were born to.

So the young aspirant, steadily for ten years or so, learned the
manners and the meaning of the noble world. He was formed. He
saw chivalry in action. He heard said and said again, "If ever you
should ask of God a boon for yourselves in this world, you can ask
nothing better than to be well brought up." "Continue! For always the best prayer you can make to God is that ye become well-
mannered." The boy was shown his fitting duties—body and spirit.

And when this courtesy writer's admonition to prayer comes
close on the heels of an admonition against noisy eating, or when
he joins, inseparably, eternal happiness and table manners, he still
seems an honest writer and earnestly sure of the joining.

3.

The School of Virtue is a crude book. It is pursuingly, unend-
ingly tedious. In substance, phrasing, and tone it is bounded between rules and dull exhorting; between—

Pick not thy teeth   at the table sitting
Nor use at thy meat   over-much spitting....
Don't smack thy lips   as commonly do hogs,
Nor gnaw the bones   as do the dogs.

(Not smackwynge thy lyppes   As commonly hogges,
Nor gnawing the bones   As ye were dogges).

Fly, ever, sloth   and over-much sleep;
In health, thy body   thereby shalt keep....
Then labor for learning   while here thou shalt live.
The ignorant, teach, and good example give.

There are 1102 lines of this. They cover about all duties of all men and all boys.

Section One tells the boy his first duty—in the day and in life:

First in the morning   when thou dost awake,
To God for his grace   thy petition then make;
This following prayer   use daily to say,
Thy heart lifting up.   Thus begin to pray...

And the section ends:

Let each soul live   in a vocation
That may his sould save   and profit his nation.
If God grants this,   Who sits on high,
We shall here well live   and, after, well die.

Having cared for the boy's spirit, the writer turns to the boy's body. Section Two tells how, after his prayers, the boy should open his day (in what *The School of Virtue* already has called "this vale of misery"). A boy should

Rise early (*much sleep dulls wit and body*); make your bed, go downstairs, salute your parents, wash your hands and comb your head (*Thy handes se thou washe and thy hed kaeme*). Put your cap on but take it off before your betters. Be sure you tie your shirt collar on tight. See to it your clothes are not torn. Fasten your belt. Wipe your shoes, blow your nose, clean your ears and nails and teeth. Then go get your book and satchel and "Take straight thy way Unto the school." Nothing is said of breakfast.

There comes, then, much about getting ready for school, and very much about behaving well there, and 700 lines on morality and manners; all tritely put and backed up by a procession of Virgil, Seneca, Isocrates, Aristotle, Cicero, Plato, and Cato—especially Cato.

This book would have had no place in a noble household. What it talks of shows it was for boys at home—day scholars at the grammar schools of their towns. On the face of it Chaucer's *Squire,* John de la Pole, Richard of York, Thomas of Rotherham would not need the primer alphabet. A horn-lantern was not their light.

We know this because we know the *Squire's* father, and the mother and father of the Yorkist King, and Suffolk's home and descent. Yet to boys from cruder ways, even to young nobles bred up scant of manners, it might (though that seems not likely) bring grace and help.

A training according to *The School of Virtue* would be far-off from that in a great household. There, training in courtesy was intimate, exact, constant, and it was highly detailed—a ritual; no matter gained on a May morning. A boy's skill in arms and the arts was to come from study and practice, and out of many years. The poor sort of behavior books told short cuts, catchwords, the obvious, the undefined and undeveloped; surface without depth. *The School of Virtue* and its like never said that mastery came slowly, or named the arts and skills which had to be mastered, or explained details of the day-by-day mastery.

4.

A book of middle quality is *The Young Children's Book*. It covers the usual wide spaces of morals and manners.

The first lines are:

Whoso of courtesy will lere [learn]
In this book he may it hear!
If thou be's noble, yeoman, or knave,
Thou need'st nurture for to have.

In the old spelling this is:

Quo so wylle of curtasy lere,
In this boke he may hit here!

At meals, the boy is told:

Don't blow on food, or quarrel at the table, or put your knife far into your mouth, or wipe your nose upon the tablecloth, or spit over the table or on to it. *For that is rude...* While you eat, don't scratch the dog or your head... And don't make faces at the table, or point, or stare with your mouth open, or sneeze or yawn or gulp or belch—unnecessarily. Don't dip any bread which you have been chewing into the common bowl.

Don't stick your fingers in a dish,
Neither of meat, neither of fish.
Pick not your ears or your nostrils,
Or men may say you come from churls.

84

Again and again come the admonitions to virtue.

> Whosoever will thrive or thee [gain]
> Must virtue learn and courteous be....
>
> Courtesy came down from heaven
> When Gabrial did our Lady greet....
> All virtues lie in courtesy,
> And all of vice in villany [rudeness].

To begin his day the boy is to

> Arise betimes out of thy bed,
> And cross thy breast and thy forehead,
> And wash thee then thy hands and face,
> And comb thy head and ask God's grace
> To help thee on in all thy way—
> Thou shalt speed better all thy day.
> Then go to church and hear a Mass;
> There ask God's mercy for trespass.
> To all you meet upon your way
> Say a good morning courteously.
> When that is done, go break thy fast
> With meat and drink and good repast.
> Bless thou thy mouth before thou eat,—
> The better shall be thy diet.

Be sure to thank God for your food. A good short prayer is:

> For our meat and drink and us,
> Thank we now our Lord Jesus.
> (fore oure mete, & drynke, & vs,
> Thanke we oure lord *Ihesus*.)

The author of *The Lytylle Childrenes Lytil Boke*—a parallel to *The Young Children's Book* and paraphrased from the same Latin —says directly to the boys:

> So, children, out of *charytee*,
> Love this book, though it little be!
> And pray for him that made it thus,
> That him may help sweet Je-si-us
> To live and die among his friends
> And not be troubled with no fiends;
> God give us grace in joy to be—
> Amen, Amen, for *charytee!*

And he ends with prose:

> Here endythe the book of Curtesy that ys [is]
> fulle necessary vnto yonge chyldryn that
> muste nedys lerne the maner of curtesy.

Both these may be taken as his pleasant declaration of faith.

5.

Books of courtesy have interest and value. Good and bad, they point out what their time judged were right manners and motives, and what were vulgar and low. The worse books show surface-forms; the best prove the deeper choices (*Manners maketh the man,* says *Urbanitatis*); all light up a part of the standards which the fifteenth century accepted. Each of the books—so it says of itself—was written to teach the noble young aspirants. Some never could have done that. At best they could only have satisfied the less with gossip about the lives of the aristocracy. At any rate, the fifteenth century liked courtesy books. Even the crudest were immensely popular; much read.

All of them asserted they trained for noble service. One reads, and doubts. Perhaps the century granted the claim of noble service—as a convention—to all courtesy books. Perhaps such a claim flattered the readers. Possibly some books were broadly written to fit the untutored boys (and the book's dullness accepted as part of any book). Possibly they were read by the least intelligent nobles; by the curious of all classes; by those who never could have served any office of chivalry.

Of course this is guesswork—cloudy shapes and watery substance, hardly sure enough for form and statement. Yet if all the noble boys at six or sixteen needed those coarser books then, as Professor Furnivall writes, what "dirty, ill-mannered, awkward young gawks, must most of these hopes-of-England have been, to modern notions!"

The young aspirant—the *pursuivant,* the candidate in chivalry—did, it seems, know courtesy books; as—to the same end—he knew the legends of romance, and songs, and books which followed the "science" of hawking. And every day in his lord's castle he had about him, to be read, the book of chivalry which was written by the noble conduct and conditions of those whom he hoped to join after a time.

7

THOMAS ROTHERHAM

1423-1500

1.

Thomas Rotherham, Archbishop of York, died—probably of the plague—in his palace of Cawood, when he was seventy-seven years old. He died honored for his goodness, his learning, his shrewd sense; for his devotion to the Church and the King; for his wisdom in things of this world and his certainty of infinite things beyond his sight; for his love of people—from the King and Queen, whom he served in good weather and in bad, to the "rude and mountain men" of his parish; for great gifts—of buildings, money, care—to the Church, to his College of Jesus, to Cambridge, and to smaller schools and churches; for his long political service (ambassador, chancellor, and the less offices) and his sixty years of service to the Church, that arched from country vicar at Ripple in Worcestershire to Primate of England and Legate; for his help to chantry-priests and country vicars—those, the poorly-paid and half-forgotten, the overlooked and unattractive, who touched the people most closely and most often; and for his steadfastness and honor when he was archbishop and when he was in prison.

The list of his qualities and success is long and may seem to damn by much praise; yet it leaves out a good deal his time has said for him. He was a great prelate; and he deserved to be. He was, too, a kindly, sensitive, learned, high-minded, remembering man. He was no paragon, but he deserves to get his credit.

His time did say good of him. The *Croyland Chronicle* holds that in contrast to two other chancellors who "became fatigued and weary with ... endless labor," he "fairly carried out all his purposes to the end."

The University of Cambridge, in 1483, when Rotherham was in

the Tower, wrote to Richard the Lord Protector "besekyng your noble Grace to shewe your gracious and mucyfull Goodness, at this our humble Supplicacion, to the right reverent Fader in God ye Archebisshop of York, our Heed and Chauncesler; & many yers hath been, a great Benefactour to the Universite.... Most Christian & victorious Prince, we beseche youe to heer our humble Prayours; for we must nedes mowrne & sorowe, desolate of comfurth, unto we heer and understande your benygne Spyrite of Pite to hymwarde; which is a grete Prelate in the Realme of Ynglond."

Thirty-five years after Rotherham's death Polydore Vergil, that untiring historian, who at least tried to be fair, wrote: "Thomas Rotherham archebysshop of York ... he was a grave and good man." The memory of his loyalty to the queen of Edward IV and her children strengthened into a legend which, a hundred years later, Shakespeare shows in Richard III.

These opinions given during his life are proof for him. So are facts assured by history. Besides, there is, for proof, what he himself has written—his will and the statutes of his College. Both of these he wrote when he was old: when he had just "completed [his] seventy-fifth year." His will (almost 40,000 words long, and in Latin) he signed on his seventy-sixth birthday, after twenty days of writing it. It is his summing-up of his life. The will and the statutes are alike in their tone and in their purpose, and some parts of them are the same almost word for word.

2.

First in his will he commends his soul to its Creator and Redeemer, to the most glorious Virgin his Mother, to all archangels and angels, to all apostles and martyrs and virgin saints, and to all those most glorious citizens of the celestial court (*omnesque caelestis curiae gloriosissimos cives*) . . ."O, if I be fully penitant, may my Lord Jesus pity me, and turn his face from those my many sins!"

"Second, because with blessed Job I most truly know that in my flesh I shall see God, and that my soul shall again be clothed forever in its flesh, through the passion of Christ and the prayers of his saints, I will that my flesh, my putrid body, be buried in the north side of that Chapel of St. Mary, in my church at York, where I have made a tomb of marble."

Then he founded his College—a grammar school, really; a college only as Eton, or Winchester, was one. "Third, because I was born in Rotherham [He almost always gives his reason for a bequest] and was baptized in its parish church, and even was reborn in that place through the water and blood flowing from Christ's side (O, that I might love His name as I ought and as I wish!), I will a perpetual college in the name of Jesus be raised there. For I was born in Rotherham. And to that place came a learned man (by what chance I do not know but I believe by God's grace), who taught me and other boys, so that, thereby, we came to high places. Wishing, then, to give thanks to my Saviour and to magnify his name, and not to seem ungrateful and a forgetter of God and of the place whence I came, I have determined with myself, first to establish one learned in grammar to teach all, freely."

Before he goes on in his plans for the College, he wrote: "And because I have seen chantry-priests staying alone in houses of lay-men—to their own scandal and to the ruin of others—I have willed that a common living-place be made for them"—a dormitory, and part of the College. "And they shall have, each one of them, ten pounds a year for living and clothes, and a room, and a barber, a laundress, and a cook all free, and some fuel." They—since "evil follows idleness"—ought always to be devoutly and studiously busy, desiring to serve God; and they should follow always the admonitions of the College Head. This care of lesser clergy had importance to the Archbishop.

Then and next, "because I see that many parishioners come to the Church [All Saints, which he was building in Rotherham, was almost done], and that many rude and mountain men—*rudes et montani*—come also, I have established a fellow [*socius*], who shall teach singing, to the end that those coming to the church may more delight in the religion of Christ, and may more often enter and honor and love His church. And I have established six chorister boys, that Divine service may be more nobly performed for ever." The boys, who must have good voices for singing and must be "deligent and fit," might come when they were six years old, or seven, and could stay until they were eighteen and so had finished their study of Latin, logic, and music.

"And, because in that same place are young men most quick of mind, not all of whom wish to rise to the dignity of the priesthood —so that these may be better fitted for the mechanic arts and other such business—I have established a third fellow, who is to teach writing and reckoning—*artem scribendi et computandi*." Such teaching was not the fashion of the time. The Archbishop here followed his special judgment.

"But since writing, music, and Latin are subordinates and servants to the Divine Law and the Gospel, I establish, endow, and will

89

there shall be over the three fellows, a churchman, one at least a Bachelor of Divinity, who shall be called the Provost [*praepositus*]; placed over the other three in the ruling and government of the House.... Thus I have made, and do make in my College, one provost, three fellows, and six chorister boys, so that where I have offended God in His Ten Commandments, these ten shall pray for me." This is a neat equation; but surely it is made in reverence.

The Provost was to be paid thirteen pounds, six shillings, and eight pence for a year; the Fellow in Grammar, ten pounds (and an illegible number of shillings); the Fellow in Singing, six pounds, thirteen shillings, and four pence; the Fellow in Writing, five pounds, six shillings, eight pence; choir boys, each forty shillings. (The diminution of incomes here gives a typical fifteenth-century scale of value.)

The Archbishop had already built richly for his College. John Leland, who saw its buildings somewhere around 1550, wrote it was "a very fair College and buildid sumptuously of brike"; small bricks, it seems, and fine-grained, and in color a strong, bright red.

"To support such burdens" he gave to his College twenty-five or so manors, farms, "messuages," tenements, "inclosures," and cottages, and the return—about £40 a year—from two parish churches. He was a very wealthy man. To set in figures a ratio between money in his time and ours has small profit. It is best to keep to comparison within his century, and say that he was very rich.

Beyond land and income, "so the Divine service may be more nobly celebrated in my college—*in collegio meo*"—he gave a shining, beautiful assemblage of gold and silver altar vessels: chalices, patens, bowls and cups and candlesticks and pitchers, jeweled and enamelled paxes, and paxbreads. A paxbread was a placque of gold, glass, wood, what not, having on it Christ's image or holding a relic, which the priest and then the congregation kissed in the solemn "kiss of peace."

He gave his College splendid church vestments. Among many others was one "of ruby velvet embroided in gold with *Vivat Rex*"; one "of red velvet scattered with gold flowers and having upon the gold of the back an angel"; one "of blood-colored silk"; others "of ruby silk with lions and trees," and "of gold upon velvet bordered with pearls." And there was a priest's cope "of green gold worked most sumptuously in gold." He gave, too, altar cloths, carpets, a mitre, and Books of the Church.

So the will draws to its end. Having settled earthly affairs, he came back to the essential, of which he had written first twenty days before. "I heartily wish and pray that my executors, most diligently and as they will answer to Christ, see 1000 masses be celebrated for me immediately, as quickly as can be after my death; to the end that through so many sacrifices and by so many remindings of Christ's Passion, my soul may be more mildly dealt with. For I truly know that my sins merit and require long, heavy punishment—Nay, eternal punishment, since they were done against the Infinite. But with the blessed Augustine firmly I believe and say that my sins cannot terrify me while I remember the death of my Lord; for in the wounds of His Body I would hide my sins, and the sacrifices of the church, flowing from His wounds, will wash them away. Through the grace of our Lord Jesus.

"This I declare my last will . . . signed by my hand on the feast of St. Bartholomew, the twenty-fourth day of August, on which day I was born, and on it I have now completed seventy-five years . . . .

"And I again do solemnly declare that I place my hope of salvation in the Passion of Christ and in the Sacraments of the Church which draw their strength from That Same. And I doubt no article of faith nor ever have . . . abhoring now and always whatever may be hateful to the bride of Christ, His holy church; for truly I wish to die—I long to die—a true Christian; and I pray, and again I pray, that so I may die. Amen! Amen! Amen!"

(This last part, in Latin, is: *quia verus Christianus volo mori, cupio mori, et oro atque iterum oro ut sic moriar. Amen! Amen! Amen!*)

3.

There is another will he signed twenty-three or twenty-four years earlier, in 1475. He was then Bishop of Lincoln, and he had just been made chancellor, and he had the full trust of Edward IV. It was his time of early, great success. He was finding he could control Parliament (no other of the King's officers seemed able to). Somehow, he kept it in session for two years, and got from it grants the King wanted for the French war. He stood tiptop in power; and he knew he did; and he had a happy confidence he could stay there. As he did until Edward died. So, in 1475, the *Croyland Chronicle* says that "all applauded the king's intentions, and bestowed the highest praise on his proposed plans; and numberous tenths and fifteenths were granted . . . money [that] amounted to sums the like of which was never seen before."

In this great success he wrote his will. It is a short (3700 words), direct, formal document; an instrument for a purpose, not an expression of both purpose and feeling. It, first, lists his "maners, londes, and tedementes . . . with their appurtenences"; next and last, it names his brother John the immediate heir.

In this will he makes no commitment of his soul to its Creator and Redeemer, and to angels and saints; no direction for burial; no charge that 1000 masses be said for him, with their saving grace through Christ; no endowments of churches or a college, and no help to any of the clergy. He expressed no love for the town where he was born in the body and even was reborn through the Passion of his Saviour; no fresh, rising gratitude to the teacher who by God's grace came to his ignorance. That is, he did not comment on the past years of his life; show closeness to any person; give help or gratitude or love to any one or any place. It is a hard, symmetrical, made will: not (like his final one) a completeness—a tree—growing by its own sap and vigor into its shape, and blossoming at times with quick feeling not to be repressed.

4.

If the final will is any measure, the twenty-three or twenty-four years brought to Archbishop Rotherham changes and comprehensions. When he wrote it, he had lived through fortune and misfortune. He had, truly, come out of tribulation. He was old, and very rich and very powerful. At last he had time to carry out purposes which had grown clearer to him as years simplified his certainties and brightened his insight into how he could best use the great possessions given him.

His last will had two purposes. It was concerned about the welfare and happiness of his people. And—first to last—it attested that, sinful and broken and a failure as he held his life to be, the Divine Goodness always shown him was, to him, "a marvel of mercy and a theme for thanksgiving that transcended expression." This Goodness was, as St. Paul said in the Bible which the Archbishop would know best, *gaudium meum et corona*—his joy and crown.

8

RICHARD PACE

1482?-1536

—a bright particular star—

1.

Richard Pace rose to his zenith in the morning of the sixteenth century. He was a notable young humanist, held to be the most learned and the most likable of the generation after Erasmus (who was born in 1466) and Colet and Linacre and More; fifteen years or so younger than they, English born and English schooled; and at twenty-three or twenty- four just home from study at Padua and Bologna.

The older men—Erasmus and the others—liked him, and were his friends, for he shared their tastes and had much their training. He was grateful to them, and looked up to them, and he expressed his feeling with youthful energy yet with deference. He knew how to be grateful. He was mannerly. He kept the right tone—without contriving—toward those so far above him.

In his earlier years it seems that he had, for those who knew him with any closeness, a distinction of character and manner and mind (a rare centering of admirable and youthful traits) rather like that which young Philip Sidney had in the time of Elizabeth, or which "that miracle of a youth" Christopher Wren had in the 1600's, when he was at Oxford. Part of this came, in all of them, from nobility of spirit, generous personality, grace of manner perhaps—from the intangible. At any rate those who knew Pace when he was twenty-five or thirty held that "for learning, wit, and sweetness of temper," and for conversation, he bore comparison even with Sir Thomas More.

2.

When Pace was a little boy—eight or ten years old—he was in a "singing school" at Winchester learning music, mathematics, languages, and whatever else was proper for a boy to know. The bishop there, Thomas Langton, had set it up. "That good leader," Pace wrote twenty-three years later in *De Fructu*, "so esteemed the humanities [*humaniores literas*] that he had in his own house a school for boys and youths. And he felt vast delight in hearing those children, at the end of a day, tell over to him what they had been told." The Bishop praised the boys who were best; "for he had ever in his mouth the old saying *power grows with praise.*"

Bishop Langton, Pace tells, "marked that I was able beyond my years, and said again and again (perhaps out of his love for me) 'The ability of this child is born for greater things.' " In time the Bishop made Pace his young amanuensis; and—probably—put him in Queen's College at Oxford. Finally, when Pace was seventeen or eighteen (all his dates are uncertain), he sent the boy to Padua, then "at its greatest flowering"—*florentissimum*. At Padua, and two or three years later at Bologna and Ferrara, the humanities—among them the learning of Greece (to him, then, newly found)—grew as wonderful and fresh and real as a sunrise.

Some time in his middle twenties he was back in England, again at Oxford. He seems to have lectured there with young enthusiasm (as Colet had in 1494, when he was twenty-seven), and his lectures are said to have been disturbing, new and alive, and intently listened to. He cut through dialectics—forms of logic—and minute phrasings and "allegory." He talked of such matters as the places where he knew St. Paul had been; or of what St. Paul seemed to him to be saying to the Church of Corinth. He treated the New Testament as a history. And he brought his Greek into use. To those listening he showed its beauty, and its power to open what had been hid.

Altogether, he was eager to find, increasingly, the New Learning; and to bring close to others, as it was to him, "this light and joy of life."

3.

Through at least the last half of the fifteenth century England was haunted by a ghost—the fear of another civil war. Henry VII when he took the throne in 1485 and the other Tudors after him faced two ghosts—the question of their right to the throne, and the lack of a direct successor who had strength to hold the throne. Henry VIII, coming as king in 1509 when he was almost eighteen, thinned the Tudor ghosts—one, at least—to nothing. He reigned by lawful succession after his father; and there was prospect that, like his great ancestor Edward III, he might have seven sons—or a dozen.

The young Henry was popular, as the Tudors commonly were. He was by all accounts a prince out of a fairy tale. He was English and young and handsome; and he was the strongest and most adept in his Court at leaping, wrestling, running, and in hunting, and at tournaments. He was the perfection of courtesy, with enough bluffness to give salt. He was a paragon of learning (At seventeen he knew Spanish, French, Italian, and Latin.) and enjoyed serious discussion; he made royally-good verses and set them to music of his own and sang them. And he was, then, the honest lover of his wife. He was, that is, eager in mind and never quiet in body because of his flashing, radiant strength. He had the energy and the directness of the Tudors, and some of the wide mind and the shrewdness of his grandmother, Margaret Beaufort.

He had in him, too, by his mother, the blood of the House of York and of the Woodvilles: that of Anthony Earl Rivers, his great-uncle (who wrote the first English book Caxton printed), and of Edward IV, and of Margaret, Duchess of Burgundy, the sister of Edward IV; all of whom by nature and education strongly cherished learning; and cared for books (as they showed at the courts in Bruges and in England), and for painting (Van Eyck and Memling were at the Burgundian Court—the "richest and most noble in Europe"), and for courtesy in manners and in large actions. Henry VIII, too, was touched with these bright interests, which were part of the rising humanism of the time.

Pace, who had become a churchman sometime before 1510, became—to his happiness—a personal secretary of the King, about 1512, when Henry was twenty-two, eight or nine years younger than Pace. Pace fitted into the Court of the young King.

4.

In 1517, while he was the King's envoy to the Swiss, Pace published his *De Fructu qui ex Doctrinae precipitur—About the Fruit of Learning*.

He dedicated the book to John Colet (then Dean of St. Paul, and fifteen years older than he, and for Pace "that learned theologian and good man") in a long, prefatory letter which tells how he came to write the book and—by facts and ways of writing—shows much about Pace.

He begins the letter: "No affairs of my own, dear Colet [*mi Colete*] could ever make me forget my friends, among whom I count you dear." He ends the letter—"Good-bye . . . Richard"—*Vale . . . Ricardi.* The letter is in Latin. Pace valued Latin, but he wrote his Latin with a difference; not writing it in solemn rotundities, but with almost the fresh flow of French prose and the naturalness of his English letters. In print today are letters he wrote in Latin and English; letters of substance and wit and learning and grace; letters easy, personal, and solid. (Erasmus, *Letters; De Fructu; Ellis, Selected Letters*).

Half-way through the letter to Colet, Pace tells how he came to write his book.

> When, two years ago more or less, I was on my way home from Rome, I was entertained at a dinner where most did not know me . . . There happened to be at the dinner one of those men you call *gentlemen*, the sort that always carries a hunting-horn slung at his back as though he would go hunting during dinner. He, hearing someone praise learning, burst out furiously: "Friend, why talk nonsense! A curse on that stupid learning! All learned men are just beggars, even Erasmus, the smartest of them all. . . . By God's body, I swear I had rather see my son hanged than studying books. Sons of gentlemen should blow the hunting-horn in the right way, and know perfectly how to hunt, and how to train their hawks. Leave learning to peasant boys!"

> At this point I could not keep still. "My good man, you do not seem to think straight [*recte*]. Suppose ambassadors came to the king, and had to be answered. Your son—if he were educated as you want him to be —could only blow his horn. The learned sons of peasants would be called to answer. And they [having answered the ambassadors] and being set far above your hunting and hawking son might tell you to your face: 'We prefer to be learned; and so not fools who boast their fool-like nobility.'"

> Then he—the father—looked around and said, "I do not know this fellow." Someone whispered to him who I was, and he muttered under his breath, and found a fool to go on talking with, and snatched up a cup of wine. When no one would talk to him, he went on drinking.

With this stirring his mind, Pace, on his vacation at Lake Constance when he was thirty-four or thirty-five, wrote *De Fructu.*

Even these shortened paragraphs from his letter to Colet show him sharply. They hold up a looking glass to him; alive; they catch his reflection; they have, in the moment, his likeness.

96

5.

Before Pace was forty, he was envoy to Switzerland and to Venice and to Rome, an intimate of the King and the Queen (who was by training and nature "a rare and fine advocate" of the New Learning, which she had seriously studied at her mother's court); Dean of St. Paul's; a learned and urbane man. So, for twenty years after 1500 he went on in success. There is the light of this eager flooding success, and of intense activity—a happy activity—over all the earlier part of his life. Then illness—possibly, mental illness—caught him. From Venice, where he was in 1522, his friends wrote to England that he would be best at home.

The last of his life seems shadowed by imprisonment, or at least by some sort of restraint, which may have come from opposition to the King, or from illness.

What Pace tells in *De Fructu* is very real. That is good reason for remembering him. It is startling to find this reality, this closeness, in the writing of someone so far away. "I ... marvel ... that he, in that misty time, could see so clearly," Sir Philip Sidney said of Chaucer in the *Apologie for Poecie*.

In writing of Pace, the temptation comes often to stop and tell how many people liked him. Bishop Langton did—well enough to make him his secretary, and pay his way for two or three years in Italy, and leave him a yearly legacy of £10—generous income for a scholar. Erasmus liked him from the first time they met at Ferrara, while Pace was in his twenties. More of his collected letters are to Pace than to anyone else. Wolsey, as a dozen letters in *Ellis* show, though not given to friendship and likings, did trust him and thought him very able. Pope Leo X was charmed with him when Pace—perhaps twenty-five—was in Rome; and he commended him back to King Henry. Queen Catherine stayed his friend. (Probably, years later he was put in the Tower for being loyal to her interests.) The Venetians, when he was with them as the King's envoy, wrote back to England their liking for him, and years afterward while he was in Venice they were troubled about his health.

Henry VIII chose him for his personal secretary. He sent him on embassies, and took him to the Field of the Cloth of Gold, and made him a Dean of St. Paul's, and held him—so it is said—"as his very self." About 1520, when Pace, just back from Rome, reported to the King then at Penshurst, the King—Pace wrote to Wolsey—was most friendly. "Aftre thys communication, his Grace sportidde wyth me meryly off my jorneye, in most lovynge and familiare

97

maner, and that doon, went to sopar, and spake off me many better wurdis than I have or can deserve."

The Swiss, to whom Pace went in the King's service, did not care for him at all, but he had said they were greedy after money and at their food, and heavy-minded, and dull and clumsy. He greatly liked their country, and came back to it later, for rest, at Lake Constance.

9

WILLIAM DE LA POLE
DUKE OF SUFFOLK

1395-1450

Suffolk's Downfall

Fortune always will assail,
And cover his bright face with a cloud.

CHAUCER

1.

In August, 1422, Henry VI, nine months old, became King of England by the death of his father Henry V, and less than two months later, by his grandfather's death, King of France. At eight years he was crowned in Westminster Abbey; at ten, in Notre Dame, in Paris. By the time of his French coronation—December, 1431—England had been at war with France almost a century—since 1337.

The first twenty years of the war, the years of Crecy (1346) and Poitiers (1356)—seventy years before Henry VI—was a dazzling space of victory. The Black Prince, only sixteen at Crecy, seemed a St. George for England. And the war was bringing riches into England by ransoms, pillage, and levies and taxes on the taken territory.

Then, in 1415, there was another splendid, romantic leader, Henry V—Shakespeare's "Star of England!" and another great victory, at Agincourt; where the English troops "without tents, bread, or water...with only walnuts for food," a French chronicler wrote, "laboring against rain and cold [it was the last week of October] defeated" twice their number. The people saw Henry V

—"who wore into battle a crown of extraordinary magnificence"—
as little less than Saint Michael Archangel, or as St. George again.
When "Early in the morning came tidings to London while men
were in their beds that the king had fought and had the battle
[it took four days for the news to come], they went to all the
churches of the city of London, and rang all the bells of every
church." When a month later Henry V "entered [London] in
solemn procession," among much else of celebration, "innumerable virgins and youths showered laurel boughs and leaves of gold
upon the conqueror's head, and sang English anthems with melo-
dious voices." England in the early 1400's still was excitedly sure
of success.

The last day of August, 1422, Henry V died, in France. He was
thirty-five. The book of the Royal Council records:

> Departed this life the most Christian champion of the church [He had vowed a
> Crusade], the beam of prudence and example of righteousness, the invincible king,
> the flower and glory of all knighthood.

It was a truth if widely stated, and—unknowingly—the mark of an
ending. For the bright day was done.

2.

The five or six years after the death of Henry V went by in
desultory fighting, in battles that did not build to any result. Then
Joan of Arc came and French success strengthened into a torrent.
To the English leaders besieging Orleans—Suffolk, she named
among them—Joan of Arc sent a letter: "Render ... the keys of the
good cities you have taken and plundered in France! ... Go your
ways into your own country in the name of God! I am sent by
the King of Heaven to drive you out of all France.... My Lord
calls me."

By black witchcraft or by the grace of God (as one was English
or French) she did capture Orleans, May 8, 1429. Five weeks later,
July 17, she had Charles VII crowned at Rheims, where the English had been the day before. In 1425 the English held half of
France; in 1450 only Calais was left them. It was in danger. August,
1450, James Gresham wrote John Paston from London: "And this
same Wednesday was it told that Shirburgh [Cherbourg] is goon,
and we have not now a foote of lande in Normandie, and men are
ferd that Calese [Calais] wole be beseged. ... Now both mortal and
immortal powers began to look favorably upon the State of
France." For France, as Joan of Arc had promised for Orleans, the
wind had changed.

"[S]he did many notable exploits above the force of a woman . . . wherefore, being accused of sorcery, [she] was burned. . . . But the French men to this day [1534] will not hear but that she was sent by God from heaven," wrote Polydore Vergil.

For a hundred years the English (as Bedford, their commander, swore for himself) had "employed body, soul, and substance" in the war, and the cost of it in men and money had grown intolerable. Trade was being bankrupt; though food was scarce, land lay unused because men had gone to the war; the flow of artificial and unproductive wealth—ransoms, levies, and the like—had dried to nothing. The Church "was greviously wounded, by lack of clerks [because] of plagues, war, and other miseries"—*William of Wykeham*. Poverty, lack of work and lack of goods, lawlessness, insecurity, lack of happiness were draining away the nation's health. England was eating the bread of bitterness.

The English—amazed, angrily unhappy, confused, helpless, naked, without a leader—looked, quite humanly, for someone to lay all the blame on; someone they could say had sold them and his honor to France; a scapegoat to bear away the sins and mistakes and arrogance and foolishness and vanity and petty quarrellings of a hundred years: one man to call traitor. They wanted an obvious and simple cause for all their complex and accumulated failures, a man on whom to put the load of their humiliations.

Unfortunately for Suffolk, in 1448 he was the First Minister of the Crown; and he had made treaties hateful and humiliating to England, if inevitable; and he had talked of peace when, to most Englishmen, peace meant surrender; and he had acknowledged—accepted and adjusted to—English defeat. He had, it seemed clear to the people, got their young King married—at twenty-two—to a Frenchwoman, and had given up English provinces to France. To come back to the center of it, he was the King's chief minister, and so the people thought him responsible for all that had happened—a natural conclusion, if not logical. Besides, at Court and among the nineteen men of the Royal Council he had enemies, who envied him and hated him, and were set to destroy him. So the Commons impeached.

3.

In impeaching Suffolk the Commons struck at a man of the highest position and power: the shining mark. Back of him was great ancestry and great connections: the de la Poles, the Nevilles, the Roets, the royal Stafford and Beauforts; great wealth; public service in England and France; high character and culture; and the confidence of the King and the Queen. Only five years before his impeachment Commons and Lords—"for honour of him in time to come"—had recommended him to the King because of the "ryght grete and notable werkys whiche he hathe done to the plesir of God."

The de la Poles were notable. Suffolk's great-grandfather, William atte Pole, of Hull, the richest merchant of the 1300's, was "for wealth and skill and merchandise inferior to none in England." His grandfather, first earl and chancellor, was for twenty years the King's minister; his father and his brother both died in France, in the war. His wife was Alice Chaucer, granddaughter of the poet, daughter and heiress of Thomas Chaucer, who was "one of the wealthiest of the Commons," who had been five times Speaker of the House, and King's Ambassador. She was Countess of Salisbury, cousin of the Beauforts, first of the Queen's household, a lady of very great position. Their son was to marry Elizabeth, sister of Edward IV. Their son's son, John de la Pole, was for a year and a half after April, 1484, heir to the English throne.

In a petition he wrote to the King (January, 1450) Suffolk gave some record of his services and of his losses since he first had fought in France, at nineteen. His father, he wrote, had died in the expedition to Harfleur, 1415. His oldest brother had been killed at Agincourt, and two other of his brothers died in France. He himself had fought for the King thirty-four years; in which time he had "continually abode in the war for seventeen years without coming home or seeing of this land" (definitely, an insecure reckoning of time). In 1429 he had been captured by troops of Joan of Arc—"the bravest warrior in this world," he said—and had paid a ransom of £20,000.

While he was in the war, in France, he had served, among much else, as admiral of Normandy at twenty-three, governor of the district about Chartres at twenty-eight, "Conservator of the Peace with Brittany," Warden of the Marches of Normandy. After he returned to England in 1430 (when he was thirty-five and the King eighteen) he served in other ways than war. He became member of the Royal Council in 1431, Chamberlain of England, 1449, a Warden of the Cinque Ports, Captain of Calais, a judge in many cases, among them the trial of the Duchess of Gloucester for witchcraft and treason (She had, for one thing, stuck pins into a wax image of the King, which she had made to destroy him.), ambassador, the King's proxy in his marriage with Margaret of Anjou.

102

At his impeachment he was fifty-four, King's Councellor, Knight of the Garter, Duke: raised, it seemed, and guarded by his great position.

But the Commons impeached him on twenty-six counts (eight in February, 1450; and eighteen, added in March). He had, the articles said, sold out England in the war, given English lands to France, ruined the nation's finances, and now was plotting treason against the King and his loyal subjects, with much else itemized into details. "Commons impeache, Lords try." The Lords heard the accusations and then Suffolk's answer, given "kneeling before the throne." The charges, he said, were "too horrible . . . to speak more of. . . . utterly false and untrue, and in manner impossible. . . . God knoweth I am, and shall be, and never was other but true to you, sovereign lord, and to your land." His full answer in the records of Parliament still reads nobly.

In the end Henry VI ("there was not in the world a more pure, more honest, and more holy creature"), though not strong enough to save him, laid no sentence against him. He "did not pronounce him either innocent or guilty, but bade him absent himself from England for five years from the first of May ensuing." So on the first of May Suffolk sailed for France from Ipswich, was captured by enemies, and was beheaded at sea. Neither he nor his wife, it had been decreed, was to lose property or position.

An English chronicle, written before 1471, gives this as a summary: "alle this lond hatid the said duke dedly." Ballads and lampoons made at his death show this crying intensity. Against him, full current, ran the hatred of the people; the shifting, unstable mood of Commons and Lords; the opposition of the War Party and of the partisans of Gloucester ("this goode man," the Commons held, "the Good Duke Humphrey"); the ineptness of Henry VI at kingship; the Duke's rivals in the Council—"most bitterest enemies . . . secretly at work against him"; and the torrent of disaster in France. There was—perhaps strongest of all—his mere accumulation of greatness. So came his exile and murder.

Suffolk's Death

William Lomner

Four days after the blossoming festival of May Day, on the morning of May fifth, the news came to London that the Duke of Suffolk was dead. To the London citizens, and to the War Party at Court and in Parliament, this was great cause for celebration. Not many, even of the judicious, grieved.

William Lomner, a young London gentleman, was desolate. He was in tears as he wrote the news to John Paston of Norwich. He may have known the Duke. Lomner came of a wealthy family. Probably, he was a connection of the Pastons. Certainly, they trusted their intimate affairs to his friendship and good sense. They saw him often. Through fifty years of the *Letters* he is a "ryht, just man," "very reverent Master," "cousin." In the pleasant freedom of fifteenth-century spelling the name stands Lumner, Lumneur, Lumnyr, or almost any what-you-will approximation.

To my right worshipful John Paston, at Norwich.

Right worshipful sir, I recommend me to you, and am right sorry of that I shall say, and have so washed this little bill with sorrowful tears, that unethe [hardly] ye shall read it. [This last of the sentence was interlined after the letter was done. His tears had blurred the ink.]

As on Monday next after May day there came tidings to London, that on Thursday before [April 30], the Duke of Suffolk came unto the coasts of Kent full near Dover with his two ships. . . . and with him met a ship called Nicholas of the Tower with other ships waiting on him. . . And when [the master of the Nicholas] spied the duke's ships, he sent forth his boat [and commanded the duke to come] in the boat to the Nicholas. And when he came, the master bade him "Welcome, traitor," as men say . . . and so he was in the Nicholas till Saturday next following [May 2]. . . . He had his confessor with him.

And in the sight of all his men he was drawn out of the great ship into the [small] boat. And there was an axe, and a stock [a headsman's block], and one of the lewdest of the ship bade him lay down his head . . . and took a rusty sword and smote off his head within half a dozen strokes, and took away his gown of russet and his doublet of velvet mailed, and laid his body on the sands of Dover. And some say his head was set on a pole by it. . . .

And the sheriff of Kent doth watch the body, and sent his under-sheriff to the judges to wete what to do, and also to the King what should be done.

Further I wot not. . . .

Written in great haste at London, the 5th of May.

* * * * *

There are at least four other contemporary accounts of Suffolk's death. This one is the most exact in details, and the most judicious in spite of Lomner's strong feeling. "Further I wot not" is good sense; what he does not know, he does not tell. The facts usually are accepted. Certainly the letter is the best written and most humane account.

John Crane

One sentence of facts, in a newsletter which John Crane sent from London to John Paston, on Wednesday, the day after Lomner had written, confirms what Lomner told. Crane comes into the *Paston Letters* only four times. He was, like Lomner, "of a good family, flourishing at this time in the counties of Norfolk and Suffolk, and he belonged to the Court." Crane wrote:

> ...Upon Saturday that last was, the Duke of Suffolk was taken in the sea, and there he was beheaded, and the body with the appurtenance [the head] set at land at Dover; and all the folks that he had with him were set to land, and had none harm.

Suffolk's Burial

That the identity of one's burial place should last on in men's memory may not count at all. Sir Thomas Browne held the wish for memory to be "vanity, feeding the wind, and folly." Shakespeare wrote once—for his own grave—quite the opposite. Yet this ignorance of place may stir interest, and tempt to speculation and balancing, and even to an inquiry.

There has been no agreement about Suffolk's burial place. Probability has been divided between Wingfield Church on his manor in Suffolk, and the Charterhouse in Hull. Probability lies most with Hull.

Hull

For one thing Hull was the home of the de la Poles as Wingfield never was.

The Humber, flowing east through Yorkshire to the sea, is two miles wide at Hull, twenty miles from the ocean. In Suffolk's time Hull was a walled town of two thousand people. At the south it banked on the Humber and at the east on the narrow Hull River, which emptied—roughly at a right angle—into the Humber. North and east, the deep curve of city wall shut it in. "Suburbes in the out part of the town be none."

It was a fortress, one of the best in England; self-contained (so, too, in spirit); "Hard to make open." Rivers or deep ditches were on four sides of it; and at the mouth of the Hull an iron chain could be "put down . . . from sunset to sunrise, in the times of war and tumult, for the security of the country against foreigners and disturbers of the peace."

Hull was the second port of entry in England. It traded—in wool and dried fish and oil and lead and grain—with Antwerp and Ghent across the North Sea, and across the Baltic with Germany and Sweden and Russia, and with Bergen five hundred miles north on the rim of the Arctic; and with Lisbon and Cadiz. It sent every year, at great profit, a fishing fleet to Iceland and whalers into the North; and its ships, following the coast, took peaceful cargoes to London and south England.

By 1400 the town was rich, well-built, proud of success. What Camdon wrote of it later was true even then. It was, he wrote, "a port of high standing, with many buildings, strong fortifications, crowded ships, abundance of merchants, and great affluence in all things." Many houses were built of the brick made in Hull (Brick-making, then, was new in England.), and "owing to the large quantity of stones brought in ballast by ships, all parts of the city were beautifully paved." The ships coming back to Hull from Iceland had cargoes of fish—light-weighing cargoes which needed the stones for ballast.

The de la Pole family was the force and center of the town's prosperity. It rested on their great trading, and on their having "come into so high favour . . . that [they] got of the King . . . many great grants and privileges to the town. It was most wonderfully augmented."

The de la Poles were proud of their town. They did a great deal for it. Merchants, landholders, soldiers, chancellors, they kept it in their minds to do it good. Kingston-on-Hull was the King's town, Edward I's, who founded it; but it was, too, the de la Poles' town, for they had brought it wealth, and, in London, had gained standing for it. They gave gifts to it—churches, almshouses, monasteries —and built in it their great houses ("palaces") and, more useful, a brickyard, exchanges, quays. Hull was their origin and their home; they were of its blood—good East Riding stock; and they had the traits and the force of those they lived among.

For five generations, the de la Poles felt a strong, tugging current of affection toward the town. The point is, Suffolk might well have wanted to be buried in Hull.

The Will

He did want to be buried there. His will says so. He wrote it only two years before his death. In it he directs that "my wretched body . . . be buried in my Charter-house in Hull, where I will my image and stone be made, and the image of my best-beloved wife by me . . . if she lust; and my said sepulture to be made at her discretion in the said Charter-house where she may think best, in case be that in my days it be not made nor begun; desiring, if it may, to lie so as the masses, that I have perpetually founded there . . . may be daily sung over me."

That is, Suffolk wills that he lie in the Charterhouse, where the masses he had established should sound over him forever; and his best-beloved wife shall in the end forever lie beside him, " if she lust." The whole and the details are said as plainly as words can say them. Such direction was a solemn charge, having in it the weight of law and of the church and of affection.

The Charterhouse

By blood and by their living, Hull was the home of the de la Poles.

The Priory of St. Michael at Hull and the Hospital—*La Maison Dieu*—were two foundations though joined under one rule and shut in by one wall. They with the Chapel came to be called *The Charterhouse*.

In 1350 William de la Pole "determined to found a most stately monastery to the Praise and Glory of God . . . who did so greatly prosper" him. He was then well on in his sixties; a very great man of his town and of England; *delectus mercator Regis*—chosen merchant of King Edward III, who in the grant of knighthood to him set down that "the said William . . . in care to relieve our extreme necessity, engaged himself and his whole estate. . . . [F] or our aid [he] most liberally expended himself and his credit." Before his death, in 1366, he had a charter for his Priory, and had begun to build just outside the north wall of the town.

Michael, his son the first earl, carried on his father's plan, but somewhat changed it. Part of his new charter reads: "Know ye, therefore, that, for the Honour of God, and his most glorious Mother, the Virgin Mary,—of the blessed Archangel St. Michael . . . with Angels and Holy Spirits . . . we found and endow in one of our manors without the walls . . . of Kingston-upon-Hull, a certain Religious House, to continue for ever." The House was a priory for thirteen monks, one of them the Prior. It was to be called The House of Saint Michael near Kingston-on-Hull, of the Carthusian Order—*domus Sancti Machaelis juxto kyngestone super Hull, ordonis carthusianorum*. Charterhouse was the easy English for *Carthusian (Chartreuse)*.

The Carthusians were a small Order, and their Communities were small. They were a contemplative and austere order, enjoined to silence and the coarsest of food and clothing, and simplicity of church service. Their House at Hull was built—withdrawn and quiet—among open fields, shut in by its wall. It stood a third of a mile north of the town, near the Hull River.

A little east of the Priory, closer to the river and enclosed by the Priory walls, the earl built *La Maison Dieu*—God's House. In the Hospital (the almshouse) thirteen old men and thirteen old women were to live; poor folks "feeble and ancient," the Charter specified. They were to hear early mass each day in the Chapel, to say each morning their prayers in it, to "resort them daily before dinner [before nine or ten o'clock, that is] to Divine service and . . . prayers." Afternoons, those strong enough should "betake themselves to some honest occupation." And always they were to give obedience to the Prior.

The Chapel was a noble place, blessed by two popes that mass might be said there and Christians might have burial. For more than a hundred and fifty years the de la Poles were buried in the Chapel. Catherine, Suffolk's great-grandmother, widow of Sir William, the King's merchant, directed in the year 1381 *(lego et commendo;* her will is in Latin) that "my body be interred in the choir of the church of St. Michael by Kingston-on-Hull [*juxta Kyngstone super Hull*], the same having been founded by the noble lord William, late my husband." In the Chapel, Michael, their son the first earl and chancellor, and his wife Catherine (the heiress who brought the Wingfield estates) were buried. So was their son Michael, Suffolk's father the second earl. That is clear from the will of Michael, Suffolk's brother the third earl: "I ordain my body to be buried in the church of the Carthusians at Kingston-upon-Hull, between the tomb of my father and mother and the altar . . . if I chance to die in the north of England." He died at Agincourt, in 1415 ("Suffolk his axe did ply," says Drayton's ballad of *Agincourt).* In Wingfield Church he and his wife have a noble, canopied tomb.

Many of the de la Poles, father to son for four or five generations, even those buried at Wingfield or in London, gave gifts to the Charterhouse. Catherine de la Pole, the founder's wife, gave "part of the manor of Miton, near Kingston-on-Hull." This she held "in fealty," paying yearly to the king as sign of homage "a Rose in the time of roses if it be demanded." It seems a pleasant kind of rental. That manor was described, even in 1383, as "near the priory of the Chartreus, on the outside near Kingston-on-Hull." Suffolk's great-uncle John, though he wished his grave to be at Wingfield, left to the "Prior and brothers of the house of Saint

Michael of the Order of the Carthusians near Kingston" ten pounds
—a very full gift. The de la Poles held the Charterhouse in their
care and affection.

The Charterhouse—Monastery and Almshouse and Chapel—
quiet, away from the town, shut inside its wall, was centered and
bounded and suffused by constant reminders of service to God,
and by the peace of faith. And everything there brought, too, the
memory and the present reality of the de la Poles, who had founded
it, and who had supported it for a hundred and fifty years "to the
Glory of God and for the poor"—*Deo et Pauperibus;* as was carved
over the Hospital door. Suffolk might well have wished to be buried
in the Charterhouse.

The Priory of St. Michael, supported by land and income from
the de la Poles and by their unchanging care, went the quiet way of
its Order until the storm broke on it, in 1536. Then the lesser
monasteries were dissolved, the Priory with its chapel among them.
It was re-established by the King almost at once, no one knows
why. Three years after that, and finally, it was done away with.

At the start of the Civil War, in 1642, the Commonwealth forces
held the town, "one of the most considerable places for strength
in the Kingdom." Their commander, "hearing that in a few days
[the King] intended to march his whole army to the walls of Hull,
and to sit down before [it], entirely destroyed the Charterhouse"
and the houses close by in Myton lane, "with a view to prevent
the besiegers taking possession . . . whence they might have greatly
annoyed the town." By cutting dikes he flooded with salt water
"the rich meadows and pasture lands on every side of the Charter-
house." Then he fortified the walls of Hull "singularly . . . with
brass and iron guns"; dug ditches "broad and deep" outside the
wall; and—beyond these, north of them—built blockhouses, "half-
moons" of earth, "breast-work for musqueteers," and "a fort . . .
nigh the ruins of the Charterhouse, on which he planted a great
brass gun." Later, the commander had "two more large culverines
. . . placed on the Charter-House battery and . . . erected another
fort" about seven hundred feet from it.

"The royalists," Clements Markham's *Life of the great Lord
Fairfax* puts it, "unsuccessful on the Charter-house side, retired
disheartened to their own damp unhealthy lines, ankle-deep in
water." Having found nothing could be won at the north, they
"attacked most fiercely" from the Humber, with fresh troops and
"two great cannons—Gog and Magog." This attack from the south
was futile; and the siege ended October 11, 1643.

There is no doubt the Charterhouse was completely destroyed. Its buildings became heaped-up stone and brick; the stuff out of which blockhouses and half-moons and breastworks and forts were made. It was rebuilt in about a year.

Whether or not any monuments were saved from the destructions of 1539 and 1642 seems not to be known. It has been said that in Holy Trinity Church in old Hull, safe behind the city walls, are rescued monuments of the de la Poles.

The Reverend John Tickell wrote in 1796:

> Between the library door and that which leads into the chancal yard, under an arch and in the fourth wall, without any inscription, lie the effigies at full length of Michael de la Pole, the first earl...and his lady Catherine, daughter of Sir John Wingfield. That these are the effigies of the above noble personages, appears from antient manuscripts; but how they came to be placed there is not equally clear. His remains would doubtless have been deposited (agreeable to the common practice of that age) in the chapel of St. Michael monastery house, which he had founded. It is possible, therefore, that at the dissolution of the monastery, they were brought from the Charter-house.

Today, 1962, only those facts which Tickell told are known; his conclusions seem less sure. Today, two alabaster effigies lie in a canopied table-tomb, built into the wall of the south aisle of the choir. The effigies are scribbled over, and gouged with hundreds of initials; the small angels which support pillows for the heads of the figures, and much of the decoration of the base and the canopy of the tomb have been broken away; yet, spite of this defacement, the effigies are noble and serene. "The male figure," says the printed legend standing on the table of the tomb, "depicts a man of striking personality, clad in the garb of a fourteenth-century merchant prince;" in the dress of a century before Duke William.

The ancient manuscripts which were said to name the effigies have never come to light, nor has any inscription or coat of arms been found which names them, nor has the legend been strengthened that this is the Charterhouse monument of Michael de la Pole, first earl, who died in 1389, and of his wife, Catherine de Wingfield. Thick uncertainty lies like dust over the identity.

The assertions are confused; are conjectures and speculations; and the confusion grows with the question: Why, if other monuments were saved, is there no record or tradition or whisper at all about the great Duke of Suffolk?

Yet the silence may have a cause. In 1539 no de la Pole was in Hull. In 1642 none had lived there for a hundred and fifty years.

The family, then, had come to its end. John, Earl of Lincoln, Suffolk's grandson, died a rebel against the King (1487); Edmund, his brother, "the white Rose of York" and so a danger, whom Henry VII held but had vowed not to kill, was executed by the young Henry VIII (1513); and Richard, his brother, the last male heir, died, by grotesque fate, fighting in north Italy, at Pavia, for a king of France (1525).

Suffolk's murder was the first act in a tragic drama, which seventy years later ended the family of the de la Poles by battle and violent, sudden deaths.

Wingfield

Within ten years the passion at Suffolk's death had leveled to an untroubling fact, or had been forgotten. After 1450 the English found their present—the final disasters in France and civil war at home—enough to keep their attention. For the next century anyone who did think of Suffolk was likely to leave him—wrongly— in his splendid tomb, in the quiet of Wingfield church, with the music of the mass about him "for ever."

Wingfield was the accepted place. The Lord Mayor of London, William Gregory, wrote, a year after Suffolk's death, that Suffolk had been buried at Wingfield. Later, Hall and Holinshed, whose chronicles made the memory for their time, exactly named Wingfield. And the first edition of the *Paston Letters* (1787) had the note: "His body was . . . carried to the collegiate church of Wingfield in Suffolk, where it lies interred under an altar tomb . . . with his effigies in armour, painted, gilt, &c., carved in wood, lying on it."

There were heretics. The second editor of the *letters* (1859) cancelled, crisply, the earlier note: "This is a mistake. . . . In Wingfield Church . . . is no monument for him."

The vicar of Wingfield, in 1925, gave the full and final word: "I cannot find where Suffolk was buried. According to some he was buried in Wingfield Church and had a monument placed over him there . . . but no remains of such a monument ever was found. . . . I am inclined to think his body was buried in the Charterhouse at Hull. [The Duke] seldom resided at his Castle in Wingfield; his interest lay more in the north."

Today, in the church at Wingfield are the monuments of Suffolk's son John, the second Duke, and his wife the Princess Elizabeth of York; of Michael, Suffolk's brother the third earl, and his wife; and of Suffolk's grandparents, Sir John and Lady Wingfield, who, about 1350, built the church.

111

John Stow's Note

"Such was the melancholy end of William de la Pole. His head and body . . . were taken up, and conveyed to Kingston on Hull and there interred in the Charterhouse." This, in Tickell's *History of Hull*, 1796, page 55, gives its authority in a footnote: *Thin. Stow.* John Stow seems part of the authority.

Stow would be good authority. His time thought he was.

To William Harrison, Dean of Windsor, a geographer and the "accomplished and informed" author of the *Description of England* (1577 and 1587), he was "my friend . . . whose studie is the onelie store house of antiquities in my time, and he worthie therefore to be had in reputation and honour." Francis Thynne, the best Chaucerian in the 1500's, an acid and unrelenting pursuer of fools who wrote books, valued Stow's "exactness and extent," and in the end, though always jealous of sharing his knowledge, even worked with Stow on Speght's *Chaucer* of 1602.

All times between Elizabeth's and ours have agreed that Stow "pursued the antiquities with equal application and judgement," and that "his only pains and care was to write *truth*." He did not ever write "for malice, fear, or favour, or to seek his own particular gain or vain-glory." Edmond Howes wrote that in his edition of Stow's *Annals,* in 1615.

A hundred and five years later, Stow had the approving admiration of John Strype, who "brought [Stow's *Survey*] down to our present time"—to 1720. Strype seems a pleasant man to have known. For sixty-eight years he was vicar of Leyton, twelve miles from central London, where Stow lived. Strype came to be ninety-four, "even yet at ninety being brisk and cheerful." He wrote constantly. Like Stow, he studied to know the old London; and he, like Stow, had affection for the older things. His way of writing is admirably his own and is exact. He turns a good and true phrase.

He says that Stow was "a curious observer of Manuscripts" and "mightily delighted" in them. He was "a true Antiquarian, in that he was not satisfied with Reports, or with the Credit of what he found in Print; but had recourse to Originals. He knew how much falsehood is commonly thrust upon Readers, either by the Carelessness of Authors, or by taking up things . . . upon slight Grounds, or upon Hearsays." Stow "made use of his own Legs . . . travelling on Foot to . . . Places, where ancient Records and Charters were: and with his own Eyes to read them." A good outline for each inquiring scholar.

Today, Stow stands high in credibility. He is "the most accurate

and business-like sixteenth-century antiquarian"; "most trustworthy"; "first authority on the history of London"; vastly above
the smooth popularity of Hall's Chronicle or Holinshed's. He still
is "the Tudor antiquary, who rarely makes a statement without
good reason."—(Letter from the Royal Historical Society, London,
1960).

Stow—to come back to Tickell's footnote—did write of Suffolk's
burial. One's clew—a line leading to the center of the mystery—
threads back through sixteenth-century editions of Chaucer. The
"lead" to the clew is the name of Suffolk's best-beloved wife.

In 1532 William Thynne published his admirable edition of
Chaucer. In 1561 Stow edited Chaucer, using Thynne's text. In
1598 John Speght put out his Chaucer, following Stow and so
following Thynne. There were two imprints of Speght in 1598,
each with notes by Stow. Stow was a friend of Speght's.

Stow wrote of Suffolk's burial in a note given in both of Speght's
two imprints. In each (on page 23 of the first imprint; on page 22
of the second), in the margin opposite Speght's account of Alice
Chaucer, Suffolk's wife, is:

> In the 28. of King Hen. 6. 1450 this William de la Pole was banished
> the Realme for 5. years, to pacifie the harde opinion which the Com-
> mons had conceiued against him. In his iourney to his banishment hee
> was taken and beheaded, and his body cast up at Douer sands, and
> buried in the Charterhouse at Hull.

On folio 430 of each imprint Stow is named author of the notes.

Through the changes of three hundred fifty years Stow has been
held sound authority; quite impartial. His note on Suffolk seems
not an inclined speculation: not a supposition made to please himself or someone else. What bias could he have had? But, of course,
what he says about Suffolk may be wrong.

Stow's effigy is in the church of St. Andrew Undershaft London
("That fair and beautiful church," he called it), close to the crowding activity of Leadenhall Street. He is seated at a table, writing. It
is pleasant that each year, for his birthday April 5, a new quill pen
is put into his hand.

The College of Arms, 1961

That Suffolk had been buried in the chapel of the Charterhouse
(as I had believed) seems fairly proved by a manuscript written
by the Garter King of Arms, who died in 1504.

From the College of Arms, London, Portcullis Pursuivant has
written me (March 17, 1961):

I have traced the MS. here [about the burial place of William de la Pole, 1450], which is one concerning religious houses in Yorkshire and the names of their founders and persons buried therein, being marked "L. 8.," ....compiled by one John Wrythe, otherwise Wriothesley, Garter, who died in 1504....

The MS. is in Latin, and [gives an] account of the Carthusian Priory at Kingston-upon-Hull....

[The corpse of William de la Pole] is said in the MS. to lie honourably buried before and under the High Altar.

It was seen from the above that if Garter is right in his account... William de la Pole was buried at Kingston-upon-Hull...

[A. S. Harvey, Esq., of Hull] has referred me to the Chamberlain's Rolls at Kingston, where under 1459 there is an entry: "Paid 35s. for 42 flacons of wine given by the Council to the Duchess of Suffolk when the remaines of the late Duke of Suffolk were carried to the Charter-house."

A Cycle of Judgment

"If anyone wept for the fall of Suffolk, it was not on public grounds." William Lomner, in London, did indeed have "sorwfulle terys" for him, but to most his service to the kingdom, his defense before Parliament and the King, whatever stood in his favor—all these, as Lomner wrote to John Paston, "they slepe."

Popular feeling against Suffolk had been intense. In a springing wave of relief and expectation (*A new heaven and a new earth!*), the triumph of the time broke into ballads and songs, which were vigorous, scurrilous, profane. One out of the many blessed his murderers. Another rhymed a mock funeral mass for him, using in it constantly the familiar Latin of the burial service:

I pray som man do rynge the belle...
And that in brief tyme, without more tarienge,
[His] messe may be ended...
And that alle Englond joyfulle may synge
The commendacioun [commitment to the grave]
    with *Placebo* and *Dirige.*

The *Chronicle* of the Abbey of Croyland shows the common judgment of Suffolk in 1450. The *Chronicle* set down events of seven hundred years—to 1486—as they touched the Community. It steadily favored the House of Lancaster, whose princes "always proved most friendly to our monastery of Croyland, and opportune helpers in its tribulations." John of Gaunt is "illustrious" and of "deservedly pious memory." Humphrey of Gloucester is "most illustrious" and "during twenty-five years . . . most faithful" to Henry VI.

Suffolk was not like those good princes. He was "a man of singular astuteness and skilled in deceiving, an abuser of the frankness and confidence of the King." In the end, the *Chronicle* says for 1450, he did "manage the affairs of the kingdom according to his will and caprice." Being "inflammed with the inextinguishable ardour of cupidity," dry with "dropsical thirst," he sold for "an immense sum of gold . . . the king's castles, towns, and estates . . . in parts beyond seas . . . obtained not without blood by the victorious hands of our kings." "However, the avenging anger of God . . . aroused the hearts of all people to take vengeance." This, in the late 1440's, was the voice of England.

Polydore Vergil's weighty, careful, almost official *History of England,* shows that this opinion lasted into the 1500's. Polydore Vergil was an Italian, naturalized at thirty-five or so in England; a churchman for fifty years—at his death attached to St. Paul's; a constant writer, and a correspondent if no intimate of Erasmus and Colet. Henry VII, about 1510, "entrusted him to write a history of England," printed first in 1534. His *History* seems fair and scrupulous —far from the partisan Lancastrian account it usually is said to be. He does not make Henry VII a "lanterne light and mightie Emperer."

He wrote of Suffolk seventy-five years after Suffolk's death. Following the flow of opinion (but it was his independence in opinion that usually was most held against him) he gave the old account. Suffolk is still "the principall contriver of . . . devilish devices"; "the worst example that ever was hearde of." Yet he tells fairly of Suffolk's end. The "nobilitie fretted and fumed for this evill handling . . . in Fraunce . . . The commonalitie in great furye accused duke William . . . that he might be punished." Then follows in one sentence the facts of Suffolk's death: "When he tooke shipping, and directed his course into Fraunce, he was sodenly taken and killed of his enemies." He gives this as common report and credible ("as meete is to beleeve"); and he adds, sensibly, "But when William, duke of Suffolke was deade, peace could no whitt the better be preserved, by reason of civill dissension . . . through contention of factions . . . which always have been and ever will be more hurtfull to common wealthes than forreine warre, then famine, or sickness."

Those authorities for the sixteenth century, Hall's *Chronicle* (1542) and Holenshed's (1577), approved and deepened and dramatized Suffolk's guilt. Hall (who knew better) calls Suffolk "the abhorred toad and common nuisance of the whole realm . . . God's

115

justice would not that so ingrained [stained through and through] a person should escape." Holenshed copies Hall. "This end had Walter de la Pole, Duke of Suffolk, a man judged by God's providence." Gloucester still was to Hall and Holinshed "the very father of his country and the shield and defence of the poor." Shakespeare in *Henry VI*, about 1590, tells this accepted story, but by his way of telling he puts Suffolk far ahead of that rhetorical patriot the *Captain,* in qualities and interest and reality.

In the next century, blanket accusations [unless of contemporaries) were less common. A cooler mood was abroad. Judgment came from restraint. Those who wrote of Suffolk set themselves to learn more of him, and from their old and their new knowledge to write fair accounts.

Two great historians of the 1700's did not agree in judgment. David Hume, tranquil and assured, for England the greatest philosopher in Europe and the first judge of ethics, turned his calm look on Suffolk and saw him as "known to have had an active hand in the [death] of . . . the virtuous Duke of Gloucester . . . this generous prince." And, since "Suffolk seems to have been a bad man, and a bad minister, it will not be rash in us to think that he was guilty [of misdemeanor though not of treason] and that many of the articles [of impeachment] could have been proved against him." Yet Hume tempers this. Of the heavy charges only one "carries any face of probability," and there is "great appearance of truth" that it was false. "Suffolk, once become odious, bore the blame of the whole . . . It is evident . . . that the Commons adopted, without inquiry, all the popular clamours . . . and charged him with crimes, of which none but the vulgar could seriously believe him guilty." Hume, it seems clear, made a cool verdict which satisfied his mind. His verdict, in the eighteenth century, stood as authority to many.

John Lingard, though his *History of England* is dated 1819, may fairly be set in the eighteenth century. He was educated—at Edinburgh and Douai—in the last quarter of the 1700's, and when Volume One of his *History* came out he was forty-eight years old. The *History* at once had wide success—accepted as "scholarly and temperate" even while it set up controversies (Lingard was a Catholic, an ordained priest, in Presbyterian Scotland); praised by the judicious and bought by many readers; and bringing to Lingard a royal pension and much university honor.

Lingard's judgment was for Suffolk. Suffolk was trustworthy; a good leader in war and in the Council; cultured, affectionate, at ease with all sorts of men; steadfast in his faith. Yet Suffolk was "acquisitive" for himself and his followers; often autocratic and too much trusting himself; but he never was disloyal to the King or had part in Gloucester's death. "I am inclined to believe that [Gloucester] died a natural death." Suffolk, in the Royal Council and in Parliament, had against him the War Party, the followers of Gloucester and York, and many enemies concealed and "devious in their ways." "They, it is evident . . . had sworn the destruction of this unfortunate nobleman." They kept the Commons "in a continual ferment." They "thirsted for his blood." "Most, indeed, of our ancient writers, borne along by the torrent of popular prejudice, have pronounced him guilty; but the improbability or insufficiency of the [evidence] will establish his innocence in the mind of impartial readers."

John Fenn, who in 1787 first edited the *Paston Letters,* says only good of Suffolk. The letter to his son is "an affectionate letter, strongly inculcating his son's duty to God, his sovereign, and his parents . . . Solemnly pronouncing a blessing on him, it concludes with a prayer for him and his posterity . . . [E]ven at this period of refined literature, it may be called a good and an affecting composition"—delightful and ingenuous eighteenth-century praise.

The second editor of the *Letters* (1859), A. Ramsay, cancels Fenn's comment. He approves Hume and Shakespeare for their truth. He goes them more than one better: "History represents [Suffolk], on very sufficient grounds, as ambitious, proud, revengeful, greedy, unfaithful alike to his king and his country." In writing the letter to his son, "Probably . . . the Duke added hypocrisy to his other vices, and a staid and apparently devout demeanor may have been adopted." This is hearing the 1450's again.

In the nineteenth century, at least in the first two-thirds of it, writers less readily gave one covering verdict. They seem less tempted to the old certainty or the old violence; and the change is more than a change in manners. Under scrutiny and with new knowledge it was not easy to make the old surface estimate of Suffolk and feel secure in it. The wish to sift away party-attack and ancient, groundless, passing gossip brought often suspended judgment—unwillingness to be quite sure on the evidence at hand, hesitation to write an absolute *yes* or *no*. Yet—at the opposite—historians of the time were likely to imply a half-verdict for Suffolk, even while they scrupulously listed the accusations against him and left them with no answers. The judgment seems hanging in the air, unresolved; in solution; suggested, merely. It is not stated, yet the atmosphere of the telling—the style of telling, the feeling with which the facts are told—favors Suffolk.

Agnes Strickland in her *Life of Margaret of Anjou* is one of the first who wrote of Suffolk in that way. Knight's *Popular History of England* (1864) surprisingly avoids direct verdict. James Gairdner, too, in his *Paston Letters* (1872-75) keeps the balance well. In telling of Suffolk's impeachment he writes: *He was accused. . . . It was also alleged. . . . It was even insinuated . . . that he aimed to displace the king.* But he ends that sentence-start with the certainty—*a charge altogether preposterous and incredible.* The complete sentence seems to show his full opinion of Suffolk, if he is neutral, he clearly is a friend. "Suffolk," Gairdner wrote, "[was a] victim given over to popular resentment."

Though nineteenth-century writers did not answer every question about Suffolk, they were ready with strong and certain words about Humphrey of Gloucester, Suffolk's opposite and enemy (and Hall's "very father of his country"). In Bishop Stubbs' *Constitutional History,* about 1876, Gloucester is *ambitious, adventurous, self-seeking, selfish, popular,* "the evil genius of his family." This *History* (though not in everything) is for Suffolk. "Suffolk was an old and experienced soldier." "However headstrong and partisan he may have been, his death robbed Henry of his most faithful and skillful advisor." "Popular indignation . . . undeservedly, had been aroused against the policy of peace. . . . If it were not for the cloud that rest on him [suspicion of Gloucester's death, he] might seem entitled to the praise of being a patriotic and sensible politician." "The easiest interpretation [of English losses] was treason, and there were men . . . to guide the commons to that conclusion." The *Dictionary of National Biography* (1882) goes further, even in phrasing. The Duke was governed by "unaffected piety and simple loyalty." The "rule of his life was to fear God and to honor the King." "His patriotism and sincerity appear beyond question."

What Bishop Stubbs wrote may stand—in the large, for there was much variation—as the word of the best writers in the nineteenth century. They saw that varying motives and acts do come even in a man of strong, centered, lasting purposes, and they took into their account that five hundred years does half-hide and blur and distort our view of Suffolk. They seem eager to be fair. They scrupulously work to find their facts, and to tell them with no prejudgment; and always to keep in mind they are writing of a man and not solving an equation.

In the past forty years historians have increasingly gone that road. At their best they show the personality which governs all that was thought and felt and done, yet allowed within itself a play —a diversity—of lesser impulses and actions, differing in strength and force as different conditions came from day to day. In such writing Suffolk is—so to say—all of a piece; yet he is touched by lights and shades of feeling which bring out different tones in the solid colors of his fabric. Such writing does not show Suffolk as shreds and patches, but as having quite normal variations of mood and of purpose. It looks for variety and, most, for the unity, the force, which in the long run governed. It tells both the important and the less, and shows which seems to be which; and it does not claim to lay open the unsearchable mysteries of anyone's life. It is willing to speculate, and to say it is speculating. So to keep the main road and still suggest lesser paths and hidden mysterious ways seems pretty much the aim and the test of such writing.

No history completely fills the definition for its time, though it has helped make the definition. Yet a good history shows when it was written—by its tone of mind and its phrasing; by what it admires and trusts; by its logic; and by the extent of its knowledge. Writing is one function of the body of an age. Each book is written in a sunlight which does not come again.

Writers about Suffolk have more and more accepted that dust and uncertainty lie over much he did, and that often his motives are lost to us. They do not use an easy, covering term ("traitor," for one) to circumscribe and define him. Yet they are not hesitant in judgment. One admirable history, published in 1955, gives speculation and opinion, and leaves an open question when facts do not bring the answer. It is certain that "To the good Duke Humphrey—an incongruous epithet, if ever there was one—war was always right." To suggest peace with France was treason. Gloucester was—no question—"fatuous," worthless in war, a tricky politician, corrupt, unfaithful to his brothers, his wife, the Council, the King, and the kingdom.

Suffolk had faults but he was faithful. He held 25 or so public offices; he may at times have shifted public affairs to his benefit; yet—this is the final judgment—two policies of his "indicate he was a politician with a conscience, if a conscience often dimmed and remote from reality." He was sure a French peace was best for England, and second he tried to make the peace which would not lessen English pride. He failed; and the people hated him and killed him; and for centuries very great accusations were accepted against him.

119

In another history, published in the past five years, Suffolk is an ambitious noble, greedy and rapacious. He was head of the Court party which was back of Gloucester's death. He managed affairs at home badly and was a trickster abroad. He swallowed down lands and offices. And he wrote verses to the Queen. (He may have written verses to her, for he wrote them to his wife, to Chaucer and Lydgate, to Charles d'Orleans—a prisoner, then, in England for twenty-five years—whose friend and custodian he was and whose style of courtly *vers d'amour* he followed.) In the end he got about what he deserved.

So the old, loose accusations have another telling. *Suffolk Normandy hath sold:* which for three hundred years had been part of the English Crown; the burial place of three English kings; the "county of 7 bishopricks and 100 fortresses." The ancient words persist. They come on again much like the pursuing lion in Bunyan's story, "a great padding pace after."

* * * * *

Suffolk has left his own words for anyone's reading. There are at least four such written records: the *Rolls of Parliament* for 1449 and 1450; his will, 1448; his letter to his son, 1450; and twenty or so poems credited—with probability—to him.

In those writings he tells of himself directly and by implication. He tells it well, for he had the gift of expression by words. He was. his contemporaries said, eloquent.

* * * * *

Because his verses are least known, here are parts of two of them, written close to 1445.

Letter

Right goodly flour, to whom I owe seruyse
Wyth alle myn hert & to non othir wyght,
To yow I wryte, *my lady*, in thys wyse,
As her that I owe fayth of verry ryght,
So ofte I haue wysshed me in your syght
As flours in Apryle bygynne for to sprede.
I recomaunde me to your womanhede.

Desyryng euer aboue alle othyr thynge
The welfare of your beautuous ymage,
Whych ys to me a verey reioysyng
To thynk upon...

Compleynt

Not far fro Marche, in the ende of Feueryere,
    Allon I went upon myn own dysport
By a ryuere, that ran full fayr and clere,
. . . .

And as I went, I gan remembre me
    How long I had contynude my seruyse
Wyth carefull thought, and gret aduersyte,
    And guerdonless, lo, sych was myn offyse;—
    The world ys straunge, and now yt ys the guyse
Who that doth best aqwyte hym in hys trouthe
Shall sunset be foryot; and that ys routhe.

Thys dar I say, and faythfully assure,
    That wyllyngly I neurer dyd trespace;
And in thys lyfe I may noght long endure
    Wyth-out coumfort or tryst of byttir grace.
    Pyte is lost,—this is a straunge case—
And forthyermore, sich ys myn happy chaunce,
What-euer I do, yt is gret dyspleasaunce.

*   *   *   *   *

To follow the changing views of Suffolk through four hundred years may seem a vanity—foam, an emptyness, dull and surface curiosity. Yet it has its interest, for the inquiry (which was to find the changing views, and the basis for each, and how well—how long —each lasted) shows what most Englishmen at one time believed about the same matter, and why they believed then as they did, and what, if anything, they all have held to, after 1450, in common belief.

Suffolk dominated his time—a short time and very long ago. His name now is the echo of an echo, or even has no sound at all.

If a man is to be remembered in any age after his own, he must bring direct new meaning to it, or must emphasize to it an old meaning, or by showing a parallel must give fresh light. Suffolk may seem not to have done any of these. In a new and crowding age he may not be paying enough for memory. Yet—at least in the last ten years of his life—he directed the course of England and, literally, centered the thoughts and feeling and acts of every Englishman.

10

THE PASTON PEOPLE

The Letters

The *Paston Letters* is a thousand or so letters and documents saved from about 1420 to 1510 by the Pastons, gentry in Norfolk. The family letters exchange news—large and small—among the Pastons; the documents—reports of agents, invoices, wills, proclamations, newsletters, letters of inquiry—touch their interests.

The news was of both personal and private affairs. The Pastons —most of them wealthy landholders, and lawyers or at leisure in London, or sometimes fighting or traveling abroad—wrote full, intimate letters. From near Norwich, one hundred twenty-five miles north of London, they wrote how they were carrying on their estates; where they went and why, and the outcome; what questions came up, and what plans they made, and their dangers and failures and success; the price of corn, and even what "a horse load of sea herring" cost (4s.6p.) at Lent. They told of births, deaths, the marriages prepared for the girls, the schooling of the sons. They sent to those in London for things not to be had in Norwich—for clothes, furnishings, what not; for, say, a cordial against the plague, never far away, or for dates, a "sugar loyfe," wine.

"I pray yw," wrote Margaret Paston to her son (1471), "sende me word qwat price [is] a *li.* [a pound] of pepyr, clowys, gingyr, and sinamum . . . ryse . . . reysonys of Corons . . . and yf that it be bettir shepe [more cheap] at London . . . I shal sende yw mony . . . ywyr Moder." Those in London and abroad sent home their news and questions and needs.

The Pastons—Norfolk or London—had interest in national affairs. The years of the *Letters* had in them violent and sweeping changes. There were, in England, from 1398 to 1486, eight kings, three of whom were murdered. In France were great victories and then wild defeats, both of which exhausted English energy, and drained England of soldiers and money.

Just after the French War ended, for thirty years after 1453, the pressure of civil war went on at home. Kings and queens and chancellors came into power and lost it. There were peasant revolts. Twice London was captured. In the shires lawlessness gained as local and central authority grew less.

The Pastons knew all this, for some were in London, and some were fighting in France and England, and those at Paston heard steadily of the lawlessness all over England, and saw it close by them in Norfolk. "God for His holy mercy, give grace that there may set a good rule . . . in haste. . . . I heard never say of so much robbery and manslaughter in the country as is now within a little time" (1462). And John Paston wrote his mother ". . . remember well to take heed at your gates on nights and days, for thieves. [They] ride . . . with great fellowships like lords . . . and ride from one shire to another" (1465).

Though the letters and documents average hardly eight or ten a year and usually keep close to facts, they make a texture of reality. They are the truest record there is of the 1400's in England.

For, fortunately, the Pastons, who wrote most of the letters, were quick-eyed, sharp-minded, intelligent. What they looked at they saw (but, most of them, not deeply), and they looked at a great deal in their time. They were religious. They believed with the faith of the age, and practiced its forms; and so, they show the medieval Church. They were not sensitive or intellectually disturbing (They could disturb in other ways.), and so, they got on—give and take— with those around them; with most people, from men and women of the Court to a North Sea seller of eels.

The Only Begetter

There was one Clement Paston dwelling in Paston, and was a good, plain hus-band [man]. . .and lived upon his land. [He] rode to mill on the bare of the horseback and his corn underneath. . .and brought home meal again under him; and also drove his cart with divers corns to Wynterton to sell. . .Other livelode nor manor had he none. And he wedded a bondswoman. Also the said Clement had a son, William, which that he set to school, and often he borrowed money to furnish him to school.

This is the only account written in the time of William Paston (the son), and it was written by an unknown enemy. Thomas Fuller tells in his *Worthies,* 1660, that the Pastons were "from Wolstan de Paston, who three years after the Conquest came into England." The choice, here, is open, for neither ancestry is proved.

This William Paston (1378-1444), son of the "plain husband," was the head of the family for forty years. He raised it into the gentry of Norfolk. He married an heiress of position; bought much land near where he was born; became Serjeant of the Law at forty-three, and at forty-nine Judge of the Court of Common Pleas in London at a salary of "£76 8s.6d." and "two gowns" (one with fur, one with taffeta); and he served—*dilectus & fidelis*—his town of Norwich, and the King. He was held "trustworthy and intelligent." In the *Letters* only Richard Calle equals him in character, or comes near. As a judge he was honored and liked. Even some who opposed him said he was "a right cunning man in the law." Fuller is sure "the Reader [of the *Worthies*] himself ... would ... have been highly offended with me, had I in silence passed over a person so deserving his observation."

He was good at business. "By some occult quality of . . . good husbandry, and God's blessing thereon," he made money and he "added to himself great estates in west Norfolk," near the sea. He and his wife (He was much away in London) brought up their six children properly for the time. He left "rich revenues to . . . his eldest son . . . and no mean estate" to his other children. Most of the children made—as life goes—good and happy marriages.

In the *Letters* he is shadowed, not shown. Only two of his letters are left and his long, mutilated will in Latin. Yet his wife—who lived thirty-five years after him—and his children and even his grandchildren quoted his opinions as wise; though there is small record that the young Pastons followed the wisdom.

Looking through the *Letters* for knowledge of him—facts and suggestions—is like groping in a dark space where, now and then but not often, one touches what is solid or sees a clear thread of light. Though he is named perhaps sixty times, most of his life is left unseen and unsuggested. One letter shows he married his oldest son to advantage. Quotations in others prove that he was remembered a long while. And the name of one of his sons and of a grandson—*Clement*—may show that he was proud of his father, the good plain husbandman. Yet in the *Letters* he is a steady, assured presence.

We owe the *Letters* to him. He is their "only Begetter." He believed that a document was the best proof. "Your father, God assoil him [Agnes Paston wrote her son], set more by his writing and evidences than he did by any of his moveable goods." (He was a lawyer.) He kept rough drafts of much he wrote and saved much written to him and any documents which touched his interests and affairs.

He died when he was sixty-six, and he (and his wife, later) was buried rather splendidly in the Lady Chapel of Norwich Cathedral. As he had directed in his will, in Latin, he was "given sepulcher at the South Side of the altar in the Chapel of the Blessed Mary in the East End of the Cathedral Church of the Holy and Undivided Trinity, in Norwich."

The Family

As a whole, they were a successful family, though they had ups and downs of fortune, and three or four times had to fight armed battles for possession. They were tenacious. In 1459 they inherited, insecurely, great wealth, which in the next eighteen years they defended in law courts and by force. For five weeks (1470) three thousand men beseiged their castle of Caister. In the end the Pastons kept it. They usually kept a good part of what they had set out to keep.

The Pastons succeeded in their occupations and professions. They were landowners in Norfolk and London; two or three were lawyers (in London, though they had more than enough local controversy); and some were at Court and in minor service to the King abroad; they fought to their credit in France and England.

The men married well. Marriage brought them wealth; children to be proud of; and capable, healthy, attractive, companionable wives of good family. Indeed, all through the *Letters,* for a hundred years, the wives of the Pastons were notably "capable"—in the older sense of having practical ability. They managed well their households, and, two of them, the family estates.

The older Pastons got on well enough together, though with some sharp-edged interchanges and exasperations. They stood together. They looked out for one another; helped one another, if at times to the acute discomfort of the one who was helped. They were critical of each other, irritable, and exacting; yet at bottom they were one in their qualities. For most of them their home in Norfolk—if they had kept its laws—was a pleasant place to be, or to come back to, or to remember.

They were good parents by the measuring of the time. In the century a child—which meant a son or a daughter not established by inheritance or profession or marriage—was under steady discipline. He owed obedience to his father and his mother. (No-where in the *Letters*, by the way, do the father and mother show a divided interest.) Entire obedience was the first law of his home.

Clearly, obedience was to be shown by acts. It was shown, too, by extreme formality of speech and manner, which lasted even for a son after he was grown up and gone from home. Always, he kept the forms of reverence, though he varied his direct obedience with the degree of his income and independence. A daughter was the daughter of her father's house until she married, when her allegiance turned to her husband and his family. *My father* and *my mother* in any wife's letter are the father and the mother of her husband.

The duty of the parents was to care for their child. It was a serious duty, emphasized by Church, law, and society. It lay within the Sacrament of Baptism. The Pastons looked well after a child's education and manners and health and morals.

Yet children seem to have been more a part of their family than a son or daughter of the heart. A boy or a girl very often (and often very young) was put for training with a noble household or—a boy—placed at Court or sent away to school or to a tutor. All eight of Margaret Paston's children were sent, for a while, from home. The Pastons gave their young children, at home or away, constant over-sight, scrupulous care; again, according to the time. Agnes Paston jotted down two items for attention when she next went to London (January 28, 1458). *Item I* was "to see how many gowns Clement [living then with his tutor] hath." She counted up that he had "a short green gown, and a short [greyish wool] . . . and a short blue gown . . . and a russet gown furred with beaver . . . made this time to [two] years. . . . And they [any other gowns] that be bare let them be raised"—sent to the cleaner's. *Item II* was to require Clement's tutor to give her "faithfully word by writing, how Clement Paston hath done his devoir in Learning. And if he hath not done well, nor will not amend, pray him that he will truly belash him till he will amend." Such scrupulous attention is steadily shown in the family letters. The Pastons formed a child for his expected future. They were diligent, and severe.

In general, the Pastons seem to have been healthy people, phys-ically strong and handsome, most of them; rather domineering; not sensitive; steady-minded and hard-working and fairly simple; shrewd, intelligent though never teased and troubled by their thoughts; not fine-spun; not, ever, mystics or artists or martyrs or reformers. For their credit they never were sentimental, miserly,

127

spiteful, or degenerate. There was an out-of-doors, natural directness about even their foolishness and failures and sins.

So they stand with the seven excellences. Their qualities were admirably central; almost wholly without excess. They went safely in the middle. Yet they stand, too, a little stolid, a little "thick"; without the fineness of spirit and understanding which brings pure sympathy and insight and strength.

Part of one sentence in Jeremy Taylor's *Holy Dying* is: "the man that designs his son for noble employments—to honours and to triumphs, to consular dignities and presidencies of councils— loves to see him pale with study, or panting with labour, burdined with sufference, or eminent by dangers. And so God dresses us for heaven." By contrast the Pastons may stand more clear. Few Pastons would have felt concerned to dress a son for heaven.

The Paston Women

The women of the Paston family in character and ability stand more than equal to the men. Two of the older women—Agnes Paston (1404?-1479), the wife of William Paston the Judge, and Margaret Paston, her daughter-in-law—dominate the *Letters* for forty years. Each, after the death of her husband, managed her household and the family affairs in Norfolk.

Margaret Paston, who was about forty-three when her husband died, trained up eight children in ways she trusted would bring them all the success their hands could hold. She gave her oldest son, Sir John, head of the house at about twenty-five, first place; as was the custom of the time. To all her sons grown and gone from home she wrote fully and steadily. She did not interfere with the life of a son who was independent, though when she disapproved an act of his or his opinion—Sir John's extravagance or his light view of business—she might say so, strongly. To her unmarried daughters she dealt—as part of her care of them—orders, advice, sharp words, and, for occasional emphasis, beating; which was, too, the way of the times.

Margaret Paston's letter to her son in April, 1469, shows her usual occupations, and her character, and her feelings. It is a long letter; fifteen hundred words long, from her blessing in the first line to "God have you in his keeping." Her affection for Sir John is clear. So is her pride: she "spoke with the Lord Scales [the Queen's brother] in Norwich. . . . And he swears by his troth he would do that he might for you." She prays, "God send you joy and worship . . . if ye be betrothed." He was, but he had not told her. She charges, upon her blessing, that if betrothed "ye be as true [as if ye] were married . . . yet not hasty to be married till ye be sure of" good income. She warns him that his old "enemies be . . . bold here," in Norfolk. She hopes he can place his sister Margery in the household of Lady Oxford, "for we be each of us weary of other." She urges him to write her, "as hasty as he may . . . for I should think it right long till I hear." At the end she asks that he send home a "kerchief of worsted" which she will make into "neckerchiefs for your sister Anne . . . I can none get in all this town," Norwich. So the items in her long letter build up the reality of her character and tell passing events.

Margaret Paston as deputy for her husband or her son made decisions, directed actions, and even set the tone of feeling there. Her responsibility went, full-circle, from the color of embroidery silks and the kinds of summer herbs for cordials to technical certainty that they could protect their house at Gresham better with crossbows, which shot lead *quarrels,* than with longbows, because —Margaret Paston is writing to her son—"your houses be set so low none man [may] shoot out with an long-bow had we never so much need." The fighting came at Gresham and Margaret Paston with twelve other people put up a good, losing defense.

Such armed fighting was unusual for her, but through every year she carried the business of the estates. She settled leases and all farm matters; sold the yearly wool-pack and barley and wheat and oats and the rest; defended lawsuits or avoided them or brought them; enforced the peace, which much of the time got no other enforcing. Besides, she had always the closer cares of her family, of her household (a very large one), and of her servants at Paston and at the other estates.

The *Letters* show how busy, how honorably busy, she was, and the affairs she was busy about. The general pattern of what the older women at Paston did and thought stayed much the same year after year, though details—the incidents—were different. At Paston the lives of these women went on tranquilly for them; as, at its best, time does go, seeming not to change yet always moving on in the repeated sequence of the years.

Marriage

Many customs—beliefs—on which the life of the Pastons was based seem astonishingly strange. One is what marriage meant to a woman. About any woman, the Pastons and the time took three matters as uncontested truth. A daughter in her father's house always was his child; a child's duty was entire obedience; marriage was a matter for this obedience. No blessing came to disobedience.

The marriage accomplished or the marriage to come was the center of a woman's life. The Pastons took that as granted. For a man to be single was a misfortune; for a woman, it was disaster. Marriage was the fixed star; the reality; the completion. The family all kept that in mind. John Paston wrote his mother in London, as a most brotherly wish for his sister Margery, "I pray you visit [St. Paul's Cross and St. Saviour's Abbey] and let my sister . . . pray that she may have a good husband ere she come home again."

Since the marriage fell so within the circle of a girl's obedience, love had small part in it. A marriage was usually for gain: a balancing of dowry against an establishment. Love might come after marriage. Surprisingly often it or a long loyal happy partnership did come.

Such affection shows in the solemn formality of wills. One man left "all to my most trusty friend . . . my entirely beloved wife." Another in his will wrote of his wife, "my sacred and high trust is in her above all others." William Paston the Judge, appoints his wife first among his executors. She, he is confident, "will act pleasing to God." The Duke of Suffolk "bequeath[ed] my wretched body to be buried in my Charter-house at Hull . . . and my best-beloved wife to be there with me if she luste . . . and [I] ordain my said wife my sole executrix . . . for above all the earth my singular trust is most in her." The Duke was fifty-two years old when he wrote the will and he had been married for twenty-two years.

The *Paston Letters* show this loyalty between husband and wife, rising often to affection. Margaret Paston, married a year or so, wrote her husband John Paston in London, "If I might have my will, I should have seen you ere this time. I would ye were at home (if it were your ease . . .) leaver than [have] a gown, thogh it were of scarlet." In the same letter she wrote, "I pray you also that ye be well dieted of meat and drink; for that is the greatest help ye may have now to give healthood." Margery Paston, after her betrothal to Richard Calle, held to her affection. For nature did break through the fixed design. The law of obedience became no law at all.

In medieval writings love is usually either a Court-of-Love self-created mirage of a Lady who did not exist, or an erotic actuality; both unlike any known marriage. Yet many in the century knew that earthly and spiritual love might become one in marriage and that such unity, based on nature, was an unending happiness and inspiration. Poets were writing of this. Such marriage shines through the cloudy, dated impossibilities of Chaucer's *Franklyn's Tale.* "For in my mind, of all mankind, I love but thee alone," is a persisting refrain of the fifteenth-century *Nut-Brown Maid,* in which a lady, her eyes quite open to difficulties, prefers a union of true love to any "brokerage affair." And in the fifteenth-century *Cuckoo and the Nightingale* is:

> *The God of Love, a benedicite!*
> *How mighty and how great is he!*
> *...Perfect joy...and trust [are his]*
> *That truly Love's Servaunt is!*

Marriage of this sort went on gaining belief and praise. Even the story of *Patient Griselda* is just the romantic and impossible and medieval heightening of, essentially, a true, lasting marriage.

Elizabeth Paston

By June, 1449, her family had found a proper man to marry Elizabeth Paston. Then begins a long account—ten years long—which shows the way of the Pastons toward a daughter's marriage, and the way of the time. Elizabeth Paston had small voice in the matter. Her mother made decisions, then asked only the approval of her son John, the head of the family, in London. Elizabeth Paston was about nineteen and attractive. Richard Scrope, the choice, was past fifty, a battered widower with a married daughter; fairly rich, and the stepson—but no favorite—of Sir John Falstolf, one of the wealthiest and most unpleasant men in England. Scrope wrote of himself that he had "suffered a sickness that [lasted] a thirteen or fourteen years; whereby I am disfigured on my person and shall be while I live."

Elizabeth was not drawn to the choice. Her mother, Agnes Paston, certain-minded, was determined to carry the match through if Scrope's property was decently large. It was. So Agnes Paston wrote to John Paston—without much truth, it seems—that his sister had "never [been] so willing to none as she is to him, if it be so that his lands stand clear." She had best marry Scrope, was John Paston's opinion, and the family's. Even her kind friend and cousin, Elizabeth Clere, conceded the marriage, "unless you [she is writing to John Paston] might get her a better." Some other one, she thinks, "were better for her than Scrope; yet Scrope is not to be put off till ye be sure of a better."

It seems all a cold-blooded, arithmetical procedure. But no spe-

131

cial harshness or ill will was back of it. Indeed, there was care: an honest purpose to assure a girl's future.

For a while Elizabeth Paston did not accept her mother's wish. Her mother used strong, fifteenth-century persuasions. Then Elizabeth Clere wrote a second time to John Paston: "my Cousin your Sister ... was never in so great sorrow as she is now a days, for she may not ... see or speak with any man; nor with servants of her Mother's; ... and she hath since Easter the most part been beaten once in a week or twice, and sometimes twice on a day, and her head broken in two or three places. ... wherefore, Cousin, she ... prayeth you to be her good brother, as her trust is in you." She warned: "Cousin, think on this matter, for sorrow often times counsels women" to desperate acts.

John Paston, after being satisfied of Scrope's holding and income, agreed to the marriage. Elizabeth Paston, too, agreed ("not withstanding his person is simple"); but her brother must be sure that "her children and his may inherit, and she have reasonable jointure." Then, for a reason the *Letters* do not give, the marriage progress broke off. Scrope—in spite of disabilities—later married Joan Bigham, daughter of a London Judge of the King's Bench.

In the next nine uneasy years the family brought out—and discarded—four or five gentlemen of, it seems, good birth and good income. "There hath been, divers times," her brother wrote in 1454, "communications with divers gentlemen." Elizabeth Paston was at home, made conscious of her failure. Late in that time, Margaret Paston, her sister-in-law, wrote to John Paston of the discomfort: "My mother [that is, *his* mother] prayeth you for ... to do your part faithfully ere ye come home to help to get [your sister] a good marriage." She added the hard reality: "[Elizabeth Paston's mother] would never so fain to ... be delivered of her as she will now."

In December, 1458, Elizabeth Paston married Robert Poynings, a wealthy gentleman of forty, the second son of Baron Poynings and uncle of the Countess of Northumberland: a good marriage. The *Letters* tell nothing of how it came about. She began her first letter to her mother after the marriage (It is written in London.): "Right worshipful and my most entirely beloved Mother, in the most lowly manner I ... beseech you daily and nightly of your motherly blessing, evermore desiring to hear of your welfare and prosperity the which I pray God to continue and increase to your heart's desire." And she assured her mother's heart that her "best beloved ... is full kind unto [her], and is as busy as he can be" getting together the money for her "jointure . . . may it please your good motherhood." Today, it is hard to know how much this is the words of a dutiful daughter, and how much is irony, or exaggeration, or a defiant flourish of freedom.

Sir Robert died in the second battle of St. Albans, 1461, fighting as he had years earlier, in 1450, against the King. He left wealth and a tangle of debts and disputed possessions, and a need, as Elizabeth Poynings wrote to her brother John, of "general pardon for some in [her] household." Sir Edward Poynings, their son, 1459-1521, became a notable man in the service of Henry VII and Henry VIII: Lord Deputy of Ireland, a Knight of the Garter, Ambassador to Spain and to the Pope, and he was with the King at the Field of the Cloth of Gold.

Then, sometime before Christmas of 1472, Elizabeth Poynings married Sir George Browne of Betchworth Castle in Surrey, a gentleman of great wealth, and one of the Esquires of the King's Body—one of those, as Sir John wrote it, "which lies nightly in his [the King's] chamber." Early in the marriage, two children, Mary and Matthew, were born to her. At Sir George's death, before 1482, Dame Elizabeth Browne at fifty became—as her will shows—the richest of the Paston family. Again, the whirligig of time brought in its revenges.

Richard Calle

Margery Paston, Elizabeth Paston's niece, has her story. She was an attractive girl, fitted for good marriage. Somewhere about 1466, she and Richard Calle, chief bailiff and "secretary" of the Pastons, secretly ("sacredly, though privately") betrothed themselves to one another. She seems to have been about seventeen.

Margaret Paston heard of the betrothal and questioned her daughter. Margery Paston said she was truly plighted. Her mother rated her, punished, and at length, in September, 1469, brought the matter for judgment to the Bishop of Norwich, since betrothal —marriage—was a Church Sacrament. The bishop questioned Margery Paston and Richard Calle separately, considered for a few days, and just after Michaelmas, 1469, gave his judgment that the betrothal stood. When Margery Paston came home that day, her mother shut her out of the house. "We have lost of her," her mother wrote to her son; she is become "but a brethele," a light creature; she is "dead at this hour"; she shall "never be in my heart." The bishop found lodgings for her with "a family of good disposition," and, after, at Blackborough nunnery near Lynn. Sir

John, her brother, was firm against her and Richard Calle; but he kept Richard Calle on because he was by all odds his best bailiff. Before this, Richard Calle had served the Pastons at least ten years. Sir John in London and his mother in Norfolk trusted him and turned to him. In eight letters written to Sir John or by him during 1462 and 1463 he is named thirteen times, with perfect faith in his loyalty and his ability.

In the spring of 1469, probably in May, before the bishop had made judgment, while Margery Paston was, literally, imprisoned at home, Richard Calle wrote her a letter. It is a troubled and affectionate and strong letter; a mature, earnest, beautiful letter, hard to match. It shows his feeling—his love and respect for her ("mine own lady and mistress, and before God very true wife"); his care for her; his anxiety about her life, then, with her mother; his confidence that she will see what is right and will do it ("I remit all this matter to your wisdom"); and his faith that, "lady, at the long way"—in the end—"God will of His righteousness help His servants that mean truly and would live according to His laws." He sees she has suffered greatly. "Would God all that sorrow that ye have had had rested upon me . . . for I wis, Lady, it is to me a death to hear that ye be entreated otherwise than ye ought to be." The lives of both of them must, he thinks, be, just then, "a great displeasure to God"; be contrary to His nature. Their way to happiness was for her to "be plain to them and tell [them] the truth." He himself willingly would tell her family, but they would more believe her. "I suppose, an' [if] ye tell them sadly [seriously] the truth, they will not damn their souls" by denying what they shall see. "God send them grace to guide them. . . . God be their guide." He adds, honestly: "[If] my desert upon every behalf is for to be thought [of], there should be none obstacle against it"—the marriage.

In the last of the letters he said: "of very right I ought to tender [hold close] and love [ye] best, . . . and so will do while I live, whatsoever fall of it. . . . Almighty Jesu preserve, keep, and give you your heart's desire, which I wot well should be to God's pleasure. This letter was written with as great pain as ever wrote I thing in my life; for in good faith I have been right sick, and yet am not verily at ease. God amend it."

The *Letters* are vague in dates; yet the betrothal probably lasted three years before the bishop gave his decision just after Michaelmas in 1469. Probably they became betrothed in 1466; wrote one another for less than a year; and then did not write for two years—

until Richard Calle's letter in the late spring of 1469. Then at once Margery Paston told her mother again that she was betrothed and would stand to her vow. Soon after that, the bishop gave his decision and Margaret Paston disowned her.

It seems shown, though again the *Letters* do not tell, that by November, 1470, Margery Paston and Richard Calle were married by ceremony. On the back of a letter from Margaret Paston to her son Sir John, November, 1469, is written "in an ancient hand . . . 'A Lr̄e to Sr. Io. [Sir John] Paston from his mother, touching the good-will of hir daughter Margery P. and Rc. Call, who were after maryed together.' " The action had rounded out. The marriage was recognized. For the betrothal could not be denied; and time brought familiarity; and the Pastons knew that Richard Calle was a most useful bailiff.

A letter and a tradition say that Richard Calle did gain standing in the County and came to have land of his own, but that he and his wife never were accepted into the Paston family. Yet in her will, 1482, Margaret Paston left "to John Calle, son of my daughter Margery, twenty pounds when he should come to the age of 24." It is certain that Richard Calle stayed in the service of the family at least ten more years, and it seems from evidence that Margery Paston and he were happy together. By 1482 they had three sons, with good family names—John, William, and Richard.

Taste

I. The Range

Most of the letters, certainly the *Letters* in bulk, show a narrow range of taste and interests and emotions. The Pastons of Norfolk reported family happenings, and their plans and difficulties, and how they were running their estates. Others, in London and outside it, told how their careers were getting on at Court, in business, or at the wars. All of them advised and questioned one another, and discussed their affairs with one another, and went over their daily actions during the country or the London year.

The older ones wrote details (but never opinions or theories) of how they were educating their children or getting them well-married. They planned with each other ways to counter lawsuits and Court influence and any other force brought against them. They talked back and forth about what they should do and say to keep a steady road—to their advantage—through the traps and loopings and violence of national changes. And daily they asked questions which their correspondent could best settle, and gave commissions of buying to their sons and their servants in town.

These were matters of fact. But even long plans and large matters were settled by fact, by practical rules, by hope of a result which could be seen and counted and weighed on the direct scales of advantage. The tastes and interests which the *Letters* show have a few solid colors and repeat designs.

Books are not discussed; they are listed as property. The Pastons never wrote of a book because it interested them, had reality, deserved thinking about and buying. Music of any sort—though all sorts of music were everywhere in England then—never comes in at all. No one says that music had touched him as an experience, an art, or even as a fact—sounds he had heard. In the *Letters* music is named, I think, once; when Sir John lists it among the "points" of Lady Walgrave, whom his brother, John the younger, might marry: "she syngeth well with an harpe."

Though jewelry, table-pieces of silver for use and display, wall-hangings and bed-hangings, rich velvet and damask and fine woolens and furs, "clothe of gold and sylk and sylvyr and goldsmyth's work" are named, no letter shows they were thought beautiful, or that they gave delight and satisfied beyond possession. The *Letters* list without comment Elizabeth Paston's "standing cup of silver and gilt chaced with flowers," and a brooch of gold: "A bee [broach] with a grete perle, a dyamond, an emerawde, apon the same."

In the *Letters* there is no blowing fresh out-of-door fun, no happy open humor, not much gaiety of mind or words. The *Letters* are vacant of flying birds (one grants a swan or so), moving animals (except marketable sheep), and flowers. So far as the *Letters* go, the sun always came up the same. No Paston shows a special sunrise; say, an Easter morning over the North Sea. The *Letters* never suggest—though they tell—that they were written in Norfolk, not in York. They never suggest the fen country, ocean air, and the misty East England light. Sir John's letter about the royal wedding at Bruges does not catch the art of reality. Sir John does not color facts with personality.

Public events come into the *Letters* as reports. Even the most important ones are set down only because they touch the Pastons. Results and implications are not discussed. Paston or Caister Manor is the axis of the time, and of the nation. Sir John's agent in London writes him (October, 1460) that "the Lord of Marche [later Edward IV; then eighteen] comyth every day to se" his younger brothers "my Lorde George and my Lorde Richard," who were children of eleven and eight; a matter of importance, for the three were close—if insecure—heirs to the throne. The report was made because the young princes were living then in Southwark, in a house the Pastons owned.

The explanation for such bareness is, of course, in the purpose of the letters. They were business letters; letters of fact; directions, reports, decisions, straight questions. Usually—for there are strong exceptions—they were sober, formal, concise, however close to the life of the writer. They were not written to convey moods, or trade thoughts about Chaucer and the sunshine, or spin out Court and Norfolk gossip. Such matters would have been impertinent. They did not belong. The *Letters* gave no value—and no space—to these. Their writers were too earnestly occupied.

II. By Indirection

A Paston letter can be reread to find—not the purpose of its writing, but the objects and the implications in it. That means looking at *what* the Pastons were writing, not at *why* they wrote; at details, not at the whole letter; at suggestions along the way, not at the one aim.

For example, one of the letters is a bill for books. Its purpose was to get the money paid. Its implication is, clearly, that a Paston liked books. Another lists with weights and values the house-silver Dame Elizabeth Browne, a Paston, owned. It is all facts, but the facts imply wealth and taste and interests.

Such reading brings unexpected reality. For read with this oblique view, the letters light up (and so bring closer) the life of the Pastons. Sir John the Elder is shown by a catalogue which lists, as his, books of heraldry, devotions, and philosophy—"sophistry"; law books; Chaucer's *Parliament of Birds* and probably the *Knight's Tale* and *Troilus;* Ovid's *Art of Love,* Lydgate's poems—unending and popular; and *The Play of the Chess,* the second book of Caxton's.

A school bill, the address on a letter, a postscript, items about schoolboys' clothes, four poor Latin verses sent home to prove diligence imply, clear enough, that the Pastons believed in education and that the boys were sent to Eton, Oxford, Cambridge, the Inns of Court, and were tutored at home or away, and were placed in the households of the Duke of Norfolk, the Earl of Oxford, and at the King's Court.

Men and women, the Pastons were children of the Church. The

Letters show, for instance, that they went on pilgrimage to Our Lady of Walsingham, seventeen or eighteen miles west of Norwich; to St. Thomas of Canterbury, one hundred sixty miles south (Sir John the Younger made that pilgrimage on foot); and once overseas to the shrine of St. James of Compostella, in north Spain. They went in gratitude, never in the holiday mood of spring or for a penance imposed. Their pilgrim-letters do not go beyond bare statements, beyond sparse allusion, but the recorded acts seem to assure devotion.

Sir John the Elder used all one letter to convince his mother, in Norfolk, that he is sending her the best treacle in London: the strongest cordial there was against colds or the plague. His purpose is to make her sure he sends "iij. tracle pottes o' Geane [Genoa]. . . . My potecarie sweareth on't to me; and moreover that they were never undone since that they came from Genoae." This is what the letter certifies; all Sir John set out to say. By indirection it tells of fifteenth-century medicine, and of English commerce and business, and of the plague, always close by year after year, and always feared. ("They die yet"; Norwich, 1452. "There is great pestilence. I purpose to flee into the country"; London, 1454. "For God's sake . . . let my mother remove"; London, 1471. "We live in fear.") And in the fresh, solicitous, happy grace of his writing is Sir John's feeling just then for his mother. Sir John does have charm, here. He always was a shining, undependable son and brother.

The Pastons lived on the edge of the North Sea. The long course of the *Letters* shows that the ocean governed the round of the year —air, sky, and land—and, so, much of their lives.

Directly, they wrote little about it. They name it, here and there, and incidentally. They got a horseload of herring (and eels) from it, for Lent; and once men from ships of the enemy, the French, "which keep our Coast . . . been so bold that they come up to the land and play them on Caister Sands . . . as homely as they were English men." Agnes Paston is anxious when "x [ten] grete vesselys of the enemyis" were active offshore. "God give grace that the sea may be better kept than it is now, or else it shall be a perilous dwelling by the sea coast." The French went on harrying the coast of Norfolk, but the Pastons were seldom troubled enough in mind to write of it.

Sea references are few, and yet it is curious that, though the sea is hardly ever called into our sharp attention, a sense of the sea pervades the *Letters,* rising out of a few, quiet phrases.

Essential

As counsel for writers, *Shun delight and live laborious days* has value. To build solidly is good. Yet it is strange how often, after the earnestness of the main attempt is forgotten, some casual lightness stays. An offhand phrase, a sudden break into emotion, catches the attention, increases pressure, and so lasts beyond the time. A by-product, not premeditated (as earnestness often seems); the lyrical, rising into high bright air; pure harmony of words and idea make alive what would have been only written.

But there must be truth in the idea which becomes bright. The feeling must rest on what is so, and be capable of meeting our judgment, and of logical defense—though logic was not thought of when we read it.

Possibly, such a by-product in writing lasts because it comes out of the writer's whole nature (of which earnestness is a part) and not from his special, narrowed purpose.

This quality which may rise to life in a phrase—a moment's writing—lasts through good prose. Style at its best is a perfect equation of idea and feeling; the union of a writer's mind and spirit; expression in which discipline and impulse are one; an atmosphere; the pervasive light. It is the best wording for the purpose.

* * * * *

In the *Paston Letters* is phrasing which flashes, sharply-focused, the writer's action or thought or feeling. He stands in a strong light for a sentence or two or three or a dozen, and then is gone, but he has proved his reality in that space. Richard Calle's letter has this light. So have other letters.

* * * * *

After William Lomner in London (writing John Paston of the murder of the Duke of Suffolk) had apologized for his tears which made the letter illegible, at the close being still overcome and torn in mind he, forgetfully, signed the letter: "By your wife, WL." He had often taken down for Margaret Paston letters which she dictated to her husband.

* * * * *

Sir John Paston the Elder, about twenty-six years old, is quite dazzled by being King's Champion in the tourney at Eltham, April, 1467. He writes to his brother, who is at home fighting to protect Sir John's property: "I would that you had been there and seen it [the tourney], for it was the goodliest sight that was seen in Eng-

139

land this forty years." John Paston the younger—undazzled—answers to the point: "Sir. . . . it pleaseth you for to wish me at Eltham, at the tourney, for the good sight that was there. By [my] troth, I had rather see you once in Caister Hall [to fight for it] than to see as many King's tourneys as might be between Eltham and London."

* * * * *

Margaret Paston had been married about twelve years when, much troubled, she wrote: "Right worshipful husband, I recommend me to you, beseeching you that ye be not displeased with me, though my simpleness caused you for to be displeased with me; by my troth, it is not my will neither to do nor say what should cause you for to be displeased; and if I have done so, I am sorry thereof, and will amend it. Wherefore I beseach you to forgive me, and that ye bear no heaviness in your heart against me, for your displeasure should be too heavy to me to endure with." The sentences are tangled, but her feeling is clear as sunlight.

* * * * *

In August, 1453, King Henry VI, who was then thirty-two years old, fell into so "sudden and terrible . . . infirmity that he had neither natural feeling nor sense of reason . . . nor could any physician or medicine cure him." Three months later, Queen Margaret gave birth to a son, their first child after nine years of marriage. The next fourteen months, the King stayed always silent. "They could have no answer, word, nor sign" from him. If he walked, he "was lead . . . silent between two men." Then in January, 1455, Edmund Clere, in Greenwich, wrote to his "Right well-beloved cousin, John Paston. . . . Blessed be God, the King is well amended, and hath been since Christmas day. . . . And on the Monday after noon the Queen came to him, and brought my Lord Prince with her. And then he asked what the Prince's name was, and the Queen told him *Edward;* and then he held up his hands, and thanked God thereof.

"And he said he never knew any thing till that time; nor wist not what was said to him, nor wist not where he had been whilst he had been sick. . . .

"And my Lord of Winchester and my lord of Saint John's were with him on the morrow after Twelfth Day, and he spake to them as well as ever he did. And when they came out they wept for joy."

This comes close to Biblical prose.

In the third week of May, 1455, "Kyng Herry the Sext . . . cam to

Seynt Albones." With him, assembled under his banner, were many great nobles, "with other divers knights, squires, and other gentlemen, and yeomen." And against him, were assembled the Duke of York and a great opposition.

To them "answered the King, our sovereign Lord, and said: 'I, King Herry, charge and command that no manner person, of what degree or state or condition that ever he be, abide here, but void the field and not be so hardy [as] to make any resistance against me in mine own realm. . . . And by the faith I owe to St. Edward and to the Crown of England, I shall destroy them, every mother son. And they shall be hanged and drawn and quartered that shall be taken afterward . . . to give example to all such traitors to beware to make any such rising of people within my land, and so traitorously to stand against their King and Governor. And . . . I shall this day for her [England's] sake and in this quarrel, myself live or die.' "

In the King's speech is his love of England, and a straight-out, English, brutal, assured defiance of enemies. "Come the three corners of the world in arms/And we shall shock them!" He lost the battle next day.

*　*　*　*　*

These paragraphs are differently written because the impulses behind them were different. King Henry's steady, royal certainty before St. Albans could not have been told in Margaret Paston's shaken and unhappy phrases. Each is itself. It has the flow and beat and lift and words which verify it.

Pageant

Some letters of the Pastons show how different the surface of the fifteenth century was from ours, when looked at by itself. There is one letter which describes the meeting of Henry VII and Philip, the King of Castile. It is all in color; twenty strong colors used about a hundred times. It lays bright patches of paint side by side, and thrusts among them shafts of crude, hard, primary colors.

At three o'clock on Saturday the seventeenth of January, 1506, a cold day, King Henry and King Philip met "upon Clewer Green, two miles out of Windsor . . . and each of them embraced other in arms." King Henry rode a bay horse. He wore a "gown of purple velvet, a chain with a George of diamonds, and a hood of purple velvet, which he put not off at the meeting," and a hat, and a bonnet. He was forty-nine years old, and ill; it was noticed that he

141

dismounted slowly from his horse. King Philip's "apparel was all black: a gown of black velvet, a black hood, a black hat, and his horse-harness of black velvet." (Drawings of the time show men wearing a tight-fitting hood topped by a hat or a cap.) Every one in his party—"not passing a dozen in number"—had "cloaks of sad-tawny" (an orange-black), or of black. In Spain two centuries later, black was still the color for royalty.

The retinue of the English King blazed in magnificence. The Earl of Stafford, a royal prince, "rode in a gown of cloth of [gold] tissue, tucked, furred with sables; a hat of goldsmith's work and full of stones—diamonds and rubies." Lord Dorset, the Queen's grandson, wore "a coat upon his back,—the body goldsmith's work, the sleeves of crimson velvet with letters of gold." The coat of "My Lord of Kent" was "on[e] barr of cloth of gold, an oder of cremysyn velvyt, pyrlyd, with a demy manche cut off by the elbowe": that is, a coat striped gold and crimson, embroidered with pearls, and having long pendant half-sleeves. One man's long surcoat was "plunket [blue] and white," his corselet gold, his "sleeves full of spangles"; another's coat was "one half of green velvet, other of white cloth of gold." *Coats* were gowns, long or short: a usual wear.

The horses—gray, sorrel, white, bay—were under heavy and splendid trappings: gold tissue with "long tassels of gold of Venice" (Lord Dorset); "goldsmith work, with roses and dragons red" (Lord Stafford); "Venice gold with a deep fringe" a half-yard long (the Earl of Kent); "crimson velvet, with tassels of gold, and bells of gilt"; "black velvet full of small bells."

It is a fine ceremony, a noble display; the flash of strong bright colors in motion. And there is in it an opposite—the King, unwell, cold, huddled in his purple-velvet cloak, and slow in getting from his horse.

When the writer sent his letter at five o'clock, the early afternoon still was for him dazzling and exciting and strange. He was amazed, overwhelmed, rather exhausted by such whirling wonders.

This King of Castile was Philip the Fair, Archduke of Austria, whose wife Joanna *la loca* had become Queen of Spain by the death of her mother, the great Isabella, just a year before. In the Channel, on their way from Flanders to Spain to be crowned, they had been "overtaken by a terrible [winter] storm . . . and, being in great danger, with much difficulty ran into Weymouth, in Devon." Henry VII had welcomed them and had entertained them "splendidly"; and he detained them with hospitality for three months, until April.

142

11

GHOSTS

"Welcome, ghosts! Welcome, poor ghosts!"
KIPLING

They are not ghosts. They are ghosts to us because we do not see them.

There are reasons for our not seeing. They are very faraway: half-way to mythology. Not much is left which shows what they looked like. If we have seen a likeness, it was a defaced image or the worn brass of a tomb, a medal or coin or seal, a figure in a faded tapestry or in a wall painting found under whitewash in a church or a garret, a capital in a book of devotions or of heraldry, the carving on a wooden seat end or on a church screen. Altogether, the likenesses are few and strange and take a search to find.

What they wrote shows clearest what they were. Yet much of this best record—books, sermons, chronicles, business accounts, letters, and even laws and charters—has been lost or is hard to come by. And, prose or poetry, it is hard to read unless it is translated, when it is unreal or has become another man's. *(Chaucer,* translated, is not Chaucer.) For in these old books the modes of thought and feeling, the customs and acts, words and idioms and allusions, spelling and punctuation, and even the type face catch and keep attention. We get small warmth and light from the book. We hardly get the book at all. Things the book has taken for granted confound us with perplexity, and confuse, and separate us from it. The living spirit is gone from it. Only a ghost is there.

So it may seem with the people of the fifteenth century. Yet they were sharply alive; equally with us. Their ways were different. The forms of their goodness and their foolishness were quite their

143

own. The forms have changed while the roots of the good and the foolish have stayed about the same. I think we know this; yet in spite of our reasoning we find those people shadows. They can move and whisper, but they are too far away from us in time ever to have been alive as we are now. It would be gain for us to break through the mist and strangeness, and find even in one person and for a moment an instant of reality. "Certes thai war men and wimen as we er and ete and drank and logh [loved]," wrote Richard Rolle of Hampole in the 1300's.

The fifteenth century in England has importance. It comes between the brightness of the late 1300's—Chaucer's time—and the time of Elizabeth. Looking into it, we may be so dazzled by the two bright centuries which bound it that it is a dark space of time with no exact shapes or clear colors in it. Yet the whole century was active, practical, strong, unique, humane, searching and changing, mystical.

More than its writings show this. In spite of its wolfishness, and hard business sense, and its gaiety and display, it was an age of faith and passion. York Cathedral, King's College Chapel, St. Mary Redcliff, the Chapel of St. George at Windsor were built then. They were built because the century had intense faith in God Creator and Ruler, and a passionate desire to find what life meant. These buildings do not speak in words. If—possibly—words are not the strongest kind of telling, yet they do tell with exactness and definition, and we are used to them. Buildings and music carry by implication. They express by indirection, not speaking straight out. At any rate fifteenth-century writing, in its way, shows the time's reality and light.

Caxton's Preface

William Caxton printed the first English book; a startling and eternal act. Before his death, at sixty-nine or seventy, he had published about one hundred. He published books he found worth printing.

He was able to do that because he had a fair fortune and the favor of the King and Queen (His first book, in England, was written by the Queen's brother for the six-year-old Prince of Wales.), and because the books he chose met the approval of the time. They were as he said "picked grain"; but they sold.

First to last, he did not cheapen his purpose or his product. In his fourteen years at Westminster, by the Abbey, he printed Chaucer and the honest poetry of Gower and Lydgate; the *Morte d'-*

Arthur; Virgil, "noble poete and grete clerk"; Boethius; Aesop; Cato; the *Golden Legend,* of all saints; books of devotion and of courtesy; *Sayings of the Philosophers*—Alexander, Plato, Demosthenes, Aristotle.

He had the test of morals for his books; as he was sure Chaucer had—his "laureate poet." His introduction for the *Tales* ended: "[May] all we who read so take and understand these good and virtuous tales that it may profit the health of our souls"; and in another place he praised books "whyche ben of noblesse and wysedom, gentylesse, Myrthe [He had pleasant wit.], and also of veray holynesse and virtue."

He kept this earnestness; yet the morality in the books was induced, not dogmatic. His choice fell—absolutely and always—upon books written "in fair language and honest terms," and "in quick, high sentences . . . casting away the chaff of prolixity": that is, in good prose. A book well-told and "touching [life] with subtylty and understanding" gave him—directly, purely, of itself—"great pleasure and delight."

He was a diligent author. Today, besides his translations there are sixty-five or so prefaces, epilogues, and comments he wrote for his books. They are lucid. Light comes through even the long sequence of words which was the sentence style of his time.

His writing is alive, quick-moving, alert. It is the sound of his voice; it carries his inflections. He does repeat adjectives he finds useful—"noble," "fair," and the like; and more than two or three times he ends a prologue with a solemn benediction which is almost a formula. Yet his writing sums up into clearness. It is purity of air, through which his meaning is quite seen.

His meaning—thought and feeling—is not hard to get, though it often is in strange dress; as Chaucer's is. Caxton's substance is as faraway as Chaucer's; as far-off, say, as the ways of the Wife of Bath. And it is as close as she is in her boldness, wit, overflowing pleasure in life, skill at her work, blowzy good looks—qualities still found all up and down the earth.

So with Caxton. The bright clarity of his writing and its lasting, central matter often bring startling close what he has written. He gets his moments of visibility.

*   *   *   *   *

What he wrote about his first book (to come back again to the center) has this visibility. The first English printer tells the printing of his first book.

And for-as-much as in the writing of...this book which I have translated...my pen is worn, my hand weary and not steadfast, my eyes dimmed with overmuch looking on white paper, and my courage not so eager and ready to labor as it hath been, and for-as-much as age creepeth on me daily and maketh feeble [febleth] all my body; I, therefore, have...learned and practiced at my great cost to set up this said book in print, after the form ye here see. It is not written with pen and ink as other books are. [It is] imprinted, as ye see here—1475; *Historyes of Troye.*

* * * * *

Fifteen years after Bruges and the first book, Caxton was sitting in his study at Westminster, with no special work on hand. He took up, casually, a pamphlet in French which he had not yet seen —a shortened telling of Virgil's *Aeneid*. What he read of the book gave him great pleasure, for it was well-written and interested him, and had good purpose. It might—he had an idea—be worth putting into English and publishing. So he took pen and ink, and wrote— as he tells—a page or two to try out that idea.

After divers works made, translated, and achieved [finished], I having no work at hand was sitting in my study where many different pamphlets and books lay about; and it happened that to my hand came a little book in French which late was translated out of Latin by some noble clerk of France, which book is named *Eneydos*, made in Latin by that noble poet and great clerk, Virgil. Which book I saw over and read therein. How, after the general destruction of great Troy, Aeneas departed, bearing his old father Anchises upon his shoulders, his little son Eolus on the hand, his wife with many other people following, and how he took ship and departed; with all the story of his adventures that he had ere he came to the achievement of his conquest of Italy...in which book I had great pleasure, because of the fair and honest terms and words in French, which I never saw the like of before, nor none so pleasant nor so well ordered. Which book it seemed to me would have much use for noble men to see, as well for the eloquence as for the histories...which history the said Virgil made in meter. And when I had advised me [had found what was] in this said book, I deliberated, and concluded to translate it into English. And forthwith I took a pen and ink and wrote a page or two, and then looked it over again to correct it.

Suffolk's Will

Two years before his death Suffolk made his will. He stood then at the top of success. Three years earlier, he had brought home to England the young queen Margaret, and with her a French truce for two years and the hope of peace after a hundred years of war.

Parliament, standing, had asked the King to honor him. The King had given him a dukedom. Almost exactly two years after he made the will, he was impeached and exiled. So turned Fortune's wheel.

The Will

In the name of the Father, Son, and Holy Ghost, one God in three Persons, Be it known to all Christian men, that these presents shall hereafter have, or see, that I, William De La Pole, Duke, Marquis, and Earl of Suffolk, in good health of my body, and in my good mind, the seventeenth day of January, the twenty-seventh year of King Henry the Sixth, and of our Lord 1448, make my testament in the wise that followeth. First, I bequeath my soul to the highness and mercy of Him that made it, and that so marvellously bought it with His precious blood; and my wretched body to be buried in my Charter-house at Hull, where I will my image and stone be made, and the image of my best-beloved wife by me, she to be there with me if she lust; my said sepulture to be made by her discretion in the said Charter-house, where she shall think best, in case be that in my days it be not made, nor begun; desiring, if it may, to lie so as the masses that I have perpetually founded there for my said best-beloved wife and me, may be daily sung over me. And [I desire] also the day of my funeral, and the day of my burying, that the charge thereof be byset upon [given to] poor creatures to pray for me, and in no pomp, nor pride of the world. Also I will, that my lands and goods be disposed after that that I have disposed them in my last will of the date of these presents. And [I] ordain my said best-beloved wife my sole executrix, beseeching her, at the reverence of God, to take the charge upon her for the weal of my soul, for above all the earth my singular trust is most in her; and I will for her ease if she will, and else not, that she may take unto her such one person as she lust to name, to help her in the execution thereof, for her ease, to labour under her, as she would command him. And last of all, with the blessing of God; and of me as heartily as I can give it, to my dear and true son, I bequeath between him and his mother, love and all good accord, and give him [to] her wholly. And for a remembrance, my great bealays [ruby: *spinelle*] to my said son. Written, and signed with my hand and name and sealed with the seal of mine arms, the 17th day of January, in the reign of King Henry the Sixth, and the year of our Lord aforesaid.

("The above will was proved on the 23rd of June 1450, Stafford and Kemp, f. 189b, Lambeth Palace.")

This long quotation, close to four hundred words, shows Suffolk's affection for his wife and the honor he held her in—"above all the earth." It shows his affectionate, anxious care for his son; about five years old then, and heir to a very great position. Because Suffolk wrote honestly and vividly the necessary business of his will, the will shows much that was true in him.

Suffolk's Letter to His Son

The day he went into exile by the command of the King, Suffolk wrote a letter to his son John, seven years and seven months old. He wrote it Thursday, April 30, 1450, at Ipswich, where he was waiting for his ship to sail that day.

Until three months before, he had been the man next after the King—duke, chief minister, royal councellor for nineteen years and Knight of the Garter for thirty, a soldier since he was nineteen, of a powerful family, wealthy, well-married, a cultured man and a writer of poetry, an intimate of Henry VI, whom he had served for thirty years in war and peace. But his enemies and inevitable events had caught him, and thrown him down, and soon—inside of three days—were to destroy him.

* * * * *

The copy of a notable letter, written by the Duke of Suffolk to his son, giving him therein very good counsel. (In the *Paston Letters*, which are the only source.)

My dear and only well-beloved son, I beseech our Lord in heaven, the maker of all the world, to bless you, and to send you ever grace to love Him and to dread Him....To the which, as far as a father may charge his child, I both charge you and pray you to set all your...wits to do and to know His holy laws and commandments; by the which ye shall, with His great mercy, pass all the great tempests and troubles of this wretched world.

And that also wittingly, ye do nothing for love nor dread of any earthly creature that should displease Him. And there as [that is, if] frailty maketh you to fall, beseech His mercy soon to call you to Him again with repentance...and contrition of your heart....

Secondly, next Him, above all earthly things, to be true liegeman in heart, in will, in thought, in deed, unto the King our most high and dread sovereign lord, to whom both ye and I be so much bound to; charging you, as a father can and may, rather to die than to be the contrary....

Thirdly, in the same wise I charge you, my dear son, always—as ye be bounded by the commandment of God to do—to love, to worship, your lady and mother. And also that ye obey always her commandments, and believe her counsels and advices in all your works; the which fear not but shall be best and truest for you. And if any other body would steer you to the contrary, flee his counsel...for ye shall find it naught and evil.

Furthermore, as far as father may and can, I charge you in every wise to flee the company and counsel of proud men, of covetous men, and of flattering men...And draw to you good and virtuous men, and such as be of good conversation, and of truth. And by them shall ye never be deceived nor repent you....

Moreover...of such folks as I write of above, ask advice and counsel; and doing thus, with the mercy of God, ye shall do right well, and live in right much worship, and great heart's rest and ease.

And I will be to you as good lord and father as my heart can think. And last of all, as heartily and as lovingly as ever father blessed his child on earth, I give you the blessing of Our Lord and of me, Who of his infinite mercy increase you in all virtue and good living. And [may] your blood [your children]...by His grace, from kindred to kindred multiply in this earth to His service, in such wise as, after the departing from this wretched world here, ye and they may glorify Him eternally amongst His angels in heaven.

Written of mine hand,
The day of my departing fro this land,

Your true and loving father,
Suffolk.

* * * * *

Suffolk was fifty-three years old when he wrote the letter. The day he wrote it he had sworn, solemnly, on the Sacrament, that he had never—in act or word or thought—done wrong against the King. That solemnity and quiet touched the letter. It is true and steady and affectionate—worth being the last letter he wrote.

A Valentine

The older men and women of the Paston family who wrote the letters were hardheaded. They had their own careers to watch out for and their estates to manage, and on their judgment, they were sure, hung the future of the young people. They carried responsibilities. It is natural that they wrote solid letters; serious stuff. Probably they looked more at their pasture to see how many sheep an acre would feed than they did at the sky. A bird in the hand would have counted more than imagination singing in the bush, if such fantasy ever had occurred to them; as it never seems to.

This judgment of the Pastons needs to be modified. What they show most often in their letters—their serious and practical qualities—is only part of their nature. Writing a letter was, itself, a serious matter. Letters were not written offhand. A letter discussed something which, for its settlement, needed exact facts and cool thinking. Even to send the letter took a special messenger, or the good luck of someone's going where the letter was to go. All these helped give recognized weight to any letter. Writing was seldom a gay diversion, a handful of bright particles thrown into the sunshine.

Yet two love stories are in the *Paston Letters,* a most unlikely place to find them. February 14, 1477, Margery Brews sent John Paston the younger a St. Valentine letter, telling him—as the day allowed—that she was his true love. It is simple, ingenuous, untaught, undemanding: a young girl's writing.

Really, she sent him two that day. She was sixteen or so, and, apparently, he was in his late thirties. Just then his family was bargaining with her father over her dowry. The negotiations were not going at all well. "Her father is so hard," John Paston wrote to his brother in London. But there was to be a happy ending. She wrote:

> Right worshipful and well-beloved Valentine, in my most humble wise I recommend me to you...I would be most glad of any creature alive, so that the matter [marriage] might grow to effect....And if...the matter take to none effect, then should I be much more sorry and full of heaviness. [In her spelling this is *then schuld I be meche mor sory and full of hevynesse*]....
>
> Wherefore, if that ye could be content with that good [the dowry her father offered] and my poor person, I would be the merriest maiden on ground. And if ye think not yourself so satisfied, or that ye might have much more good (as I have understood by your afore), [then I pray you] good, true, and loving Valentine, that ye take no such labour upon you as to come more for that matter, but let it pass and never more be spoken of, as I may be your true lover and beadswoman during my life. No more unto you at this time, but Almighty Jesus preserve you, both body and soul.

The letter, strange in wording, seems to bring close what the young girl felt.

Statute of a College
...as from a spring...

When he was seventy-five, Archbishop Rotherham founded his College of Jesus, at the town where he was born. In the Statutes which he wrote as laws of the College and counsel to its ten teachers he gives his praise to God, and tells his affection for the town and his gratitude to one man who taught him when he was a boy "unlettered and rude."

He begins the Statutes, which are in Latin: "To all the sons of Holy Mother Church . . . Thomas, by divine permission, Archbishop of York, Primate of England, and Legate from the Apostolic See, saluting, with embraces of the Lord. *Whereas,* we, the archbishop foresaid, weighing and considering that in the town of Rotherham, in our diocese of York, where we were born and by the font of holy regeneration [by the Sacrament of Baptism] were born again; where also, with others, [we were] passing our youth without letters; and should have remained so untaught and unlettered and rude to a greater age but that by the grace of God a man learned in grammar came there, by whom we drank of learning as from a spring. *Therefore,* desiring to render thanks to the Saviour, and not to seem ungrateful nor show ourselves unmindful of the benefits of God and of the place whence we came, we have determined to cause a like fountain to flow there; that is, to establish a teacher of grammar there for ever."

Even through the unfamiliar medieval Latin of the Statutes his gratitude shows true and fresh and strong.

ENDING

... this insubstantial pageant faded,
Leave not a rack behind   TEMPEST

I suppose one does not readily know a time that has passed. He cannot gain its intimacy; cannot accept it without effort. The look of fields and streets five hundred years ago, food on the tables, clothing, the sound of the constant church bells—all the colors and lights and shades of usual, outward life are immeasurably far away. Its talk takes strange turns of phrase and very strange pronouncing, and is muffled by distance. People stand as shadows, or waver like overbright figures in a tapestry. The time seems an insubstantial pageant.

Yet the pageant leaves more than a rack behind, more than shining clouds that thin to nothing.

It is the details which seem most strange, not the forces which directed them—affection or hate, rational beliefs, the body's appetites, the faith of the spirit. I mean that, say, Suffolk's downfall—the party enmity, the attacks on him, his destruction—has been fairly often repeated in history. We can parallel each part of it. Only the old forms are different: the five strokes of a rusty sword; his body and his head cast on Dover sands. Suffolk's love for his son, his solicitude and confidence and affection for his wife (more real and lasting than the violent acts) come clearly through the dust and strangeness of his will.

So it seems with other records of the time.